Praise for *Iraq: The Logic of Withdrawal*

"*Iraq: The Logic of Withdrawal* is an urgent book, a complete manual for those who wish to resist the occupation. I hope it becomes an effective tool in the hands of those who have the guts to stand up and be counted."

—Arundhati Roy

"A powerful and compelling argument on behalf of withdrawal from Iraq. An important book that every American should read!"

—Ron Kovic

"Any U.S. service member willing to kill or be killed in Iraq should read Anthony Arnove's *Iraq: The Logic of Withdrawal*. While offering a historical analysis of imperial intervention, the book is an easy-to-read, uncorrupted account of the events that led to the criminal U.S. invasion and occupation of Iraq and of why it only makes sense to withdraw all foreign troops from there immediately."

—Camilo Mejía

"How can the military occupation of Iraq that resulted from an illegal and immoral invasion bring anything but more hatred, chaos, and death? As thousands of lives continue to be lost, as more of Iraq is devoured by U.S. corporations, as the sovereignty of the Iraqi people is undermined daily, and the rights and safety of Iraqi women are destroyed, Anthony Arnove makes a impassioned, unflinching case for immediate U.S. withdrawal. Read this book and bring the troops home now."

—Eve Ensler

"Anthony Arnove has written a book that every American, regardless of political viewpoint, should read. It brings historical awareness, evidence, and reason to bear in mounting an overwhelmingly persuasive and lucid argument for an immediate American withdrawal from Iraq. Heeding Arnove's assessment would create the possibility of an

American political renewal. Ignoring it, as the mainstream seems stubbornly determined to do, is to open wide a gateway to disaster."

—Richard Falk

"A compelling and courageous call to do the only right thing: bring the troops home now!"

—Mike Davis

"It is the occupation of Iraq that has created the savage chaos. A withdrawal of all Western troops is a prerequisite of self-determination. Anthony Arnove's arguments are persuasive and his logic undeniable."

—Tariq Ali

"The hidden obstacle to U.S. withdrawal from Vietnam was liberal America's resistance to the notion of a deliberately rapacious act of invasion, preferring the lie of the bungling giant being drawn into a 'quagmire.' The same is true of Iraq today, which makes this insightful book a must read for those who believe the truth matters."

—John Pilger

"Arnove accurately and eloquently dispels the myths of U.S. benevolence and victory in Iraq. His assessment of the situation on the ground is as accurate and gripping as any I've seen, while providing a searing testimony about the total failure of the illegal invasion and occupation and why the only true solution is a full and immediate U.S. withdrawal."

—Dahr Jamail

"The war in Iraq was a criminal one and a disastrous mistake. Yet, worse than that, it was unsurprising, belonging to a train of thought that has dominated certain Western policies for a century or more. This furious book reveals how and why this is so. Essential reading."

—John Berger

"Anthony Arnove's *Iraq: The Logic of Withdrawal* is timely and is urgently needed. As the demand grows for immediate withdrawal, this cogently argued text will help popular pressure rise to the point that it cannot be ignored."

—Dennis Brutus

"There is no exit door? The authors of this serial killing should have, at least, the minimal decency to invent it. 'And death shall have no dominion...'"

—Eduardo Galeano

"Arnove challenges the absurdity and high human cost of the U.S. war on Iraq in clear and irrefutable terms in this book."

—Elaine Hagopian

"This is the most convincing case made for the immediate end of U.S. occupation. As the occupation drags, on, Arnove's call will be remembered as an important warning. All those who care about peace and justice should read this book. This book is not only an important analysis of U.S. war and occupation, but it can also serve as a primer for activists around the world."

—As'ad AbuKhalil

"Anthony Arnove's *Iraq: The Logic of Withdrawal* is an excellent handbook, displaying in a well-written, easy-to-read form all the key arguments for the immediate, total, and unconditional withdrawal of U.S. and allied occupation troops from Iraq. It is a most precious and timely contribution to the building of the antiwar movement."

—Gilbert Achcar

"*Iraq: The Logic of Withdrawal* strongly and persuasively demonstrates that the immediate termination of the military occupation of Iraq and withdrawal of U.S. forces would not only serve U.S. interests, but Iraqi interest as well. It reveals the manner in which the strategic landscape of the entire region has been reshaped by this imperial war, and it debunks the myth that a withdrawal now would create a vacuum and ignite a civil war, when indeed a civil war is already ongoing as a result of the invasion and occupation. It is a must read for those who want to learn about how the United States is trying to recolonize the Arab world."

—Naseer Aruri

"A decade ago, with Bill Clinton in the White House, Arnove helped wake us up to the horrors of the U.S.-led economic sanctions against Iraq. Today, he is sounding the alarm against the bipartisan myth of benevolent occupation. His is a rare and credible voice of sanity in the most insane of times."

—Jeremy Scahill

"Nothing could be more policy-relevant today than Anthony Arnove's analysis in this book."

—Edward S. Herman

"As the global antiwar movement wrestles with the aftermath of the Iraq invasion, Anthony Arnove's rigorous and well-informed arguments for an immediate withdrawal are timely and necessary. He strips away the dangerous illusions that prop up the notion that the U.S. occupation can in any way benefit the Iraqi people."

—Mike Marqusee

IRAQ
THE LOGIC OF WITHDRAWAL

Other books by Anthony Arnove

Iraq Under Siege: The Deadly Impact of Sanctions and War

Terrorism and War
(with Howard Zinn)

Voices of a People's History of the United States
(with Howard Zinn)

IRAQ

The Logic of Withdrawal

Anthony Arnove

THE NEW PRESS

NEW YORK
LONDON

Requests for permission to reproduce selections from this book
should be mailed to: Permissions Department,
The New Press, 38 Greene Street, New York, NY 10013

Published in the United States by The New Press, New York, 2006
Distributed by W. W. Norton & Company, Inc., New York

LIBRARY OF CONGRESS CATALOGING-IN-PUBLICATION DATA

Arnove, Anthony, 1969–
Iraq : the logic of withdrawal / Anthony Arnove ; foreword and afterword
by Howard Zinn.
p.   cm.
Includes bibliographical references and index.
ISBN-13: 978-1-59558-079-5 (hc.)
ISBN-10: 1-59558-079-4 (hc.)
1. Iraq War, 2003–   2. Iraq war, 2003—Occupied territories.   3. Insurgency—Iraq.
4. United States—Politics and government—2001–   I. Title.

DS79.76.A76   2006
956.7044'31—dc22   2005058422

The New Press was established in 1990 as a not-for-profit alternative to the large,
commercial publishing houses currently dominating the book publishing
industry. The New Press operates in the public interest rather than for private gain,
and is committed to publishing, in innovative ways, works of educational, cultural,
and community value that are often deemed insufficiently profitable.

www.thenewpress.com

Composition by dix!
This book was set in Minion

Printed in the United States of America

2   4   6   8   10   9   7   5   3   1

CONTENTS

FOREWORD
by Howard Zinn

IT IS STRIKING, and an unhappy commentary on our nation, that
no major political figure, no major newspaper, has had the courage
or the wisdom or the will to say what should by now be obvious: that
we must withdraw our military from Iraq, and the sooner the better.
The reason is simple: our presence there is a disaster for the U.S.
people and an even bigger disaster for the Iraqi people.

It is a strange logic to declare, as so many in Washington and in
the major media do, that it was wrong for us to invade Iraq but right
for us to remain. A recent *New York Times* editorial, headed "Grim
Realities in Iraq," sums up the situation accurately: "Some twenty-
one months after the American invasion, United States military
forces remain essentially alone in battling what seems to be a growing insurgency, with no clear prospect of decisive success any time in
the foreseeable future." And then, in an extraordinary non sequitur,
"Given the lack of other countries willing to put up their hands as
volunteers, the only answer seems to be more American troops, and
not just through the spring, as currently planned. . . . Forces need to
be expanded through stepped-up recruitment."[1]

Here is the logic: "We are alone in the world in this invasion. The
insurgency is growing. There is no visible prospect of success.

Therefore let's send more troops." Is this not the definition of fanaticism (or is *fantasy* a better word?)—that when you discover you are going in the wrong direction, you redouble your speed?

In all of this, there is an unexamined premise: that military victory would constitute "success." Conceivably the United States, possessed of enormous weaponry, might finally crush the resistance in Iraq. The cost would be great. Already tens of thousands, perhaps a hundred thousand, have lost their lives (and we must not differentiate between "their" casualties and "ours" if we believe all human beings have an equal right to life). Would that be a "success"?

Two years into the American escalation in Vietnam, in the spring of 1967, I wrote a book called *Vietnam: The Logic of Withdrawal.*[2] It was the first book on the war to urge an immediate departure from Southeast Asia, and at that time I heard the same arguments against withdrawal that we are hearing now. The United States did not pull out its troops for six more years. In those years at least a million more Vietnamese, and perhaps thirty thousand U.S. military, were killed.

"We must stay in Iraq," it is said again and again, so that we can bring stability and democracy to that country. Isn't it clear that after three years of war and occupation, we have brought only chaos, violence, and death to that country, and have no prospect of creating democracy? Can democracy be nurtured by destroying cities, by bombing, by driving people from their homes?

There is no certainty as to what would happen in our absence, but there is absolute certainty about the result of our presence: escalating deaths on both sides. Mostly, the loss of life is among Iraqi civilians, many of them children. But even the smaller casualty toll on the U.S. side includes thousands of maimed soldiers, some losing limbs, others blinded. And tens of thousands face psychological damage in the aftermath.

Have we learned nothing from the history of imperial occupations, all pretending to help the people being occupied?

The United States, the latest of the great empires, is perhaps the most self-deluded, having forgotten that history, including our own. Did our fifty-year occupation of the Philippines, or our long occupations of Haiti (1915–1934) and the Dominican Republic (1916–1924), or our military interventions in Southeast Asia and the Caribbean throughout the twentieth century bring democracy to those places?

Our military presence in Iraq is hurting, not helping. It is angering people around the world, and therefore magnifying the danger of terrorism. Far from making the United States safer, as Bush has claimed, it has increased the chance that enraged people will strike us here.

In withdrawing our troops, we can improve the odds of peace and stability (leaving aside the delusion of "democracy") in Iraq. We mustn't underestimate the capacity of the Iraqis, once free of both Saddam Hussein and foreign occupation, to forge their own future.

But the first step is to support our troops in the only way the word *support* can have real meaning—by saving their lives, their limbs, their sanity, by bringing them home.

INTRODUCTION

IN THIS BOOK, I argue the case for the immediate withdrawal of all U.S. and international troops from Iraq. I stress immediate withdrawal, as opposed to various proposals for a timetable for withdrawal, gradual withdrawal, or withdrawal when the situation in Iraq has "stabilized" at some undefined point in the future. All of these, in the end, are recipes for continued occupation and bloodshed, for one simple reason: the people who will decide when the U.S. military and its allies are prepared to leave are the very people who started the war in the first place and now have so much at stake in winning it.

The title of this book is borrowed from Howard Zinn's prescient *Vietnam: The Logic of Withdrawal*, first published in 1967 by Beacon Press and republished in 2002 by South End Press.[1] In that book, Zinn made a clear and convincing case for the immediate withdrawal of U.S. troops from Vietnam. In retrospect, we can see the enormous suffering caused by prolonging that war. As it became clear that the United States was losing in Vietnam, Washington did not at first retreat, but expanded the war to Laos and Cambodia. Tens of thousands more U.S. soldiers and literally millions of people in Indochina would die before the government finally was forced to withdraw all of its troops.

No historical analogies are ever exact, but the parallels between Iraq and Vietnam are significant. In both cases, the greatest military power in human history has encountered the limits of its ability to impose its will on a people who do not welcome its intervention. In Iraq, like Vietnam, soldiers themselves have begun to question the rationale for the war given by politicians and daily echoed by the dominant media, as they see on the ground the enormous contradictions in the claim that the United States is "bringing democracy" to a people it is brutalizing and repressing. In both cases, the war abroad is having profound costs at home, in terms of slashed social spending, families and communities torn apart by the war, and veterans abandoned by a government that seeks to silence dissent with its empty slogans insisting that we must "support our troops," by which they mean we must uncritically support the war that is killing and maiming them needlessly. Today, the United States is also attempting to cover for its failures by pursuing an "Iraqization" of the conflict, much as it pursued "Vietnamization" before.

In many ways, though, the analogy to Vietnam understates what is at stake for the U.S. government in Iraq. In geostrategic terms, Iraq, which has the world's second-largest oil reserves and sits in a region with two thirds of global oil reserves, is far more important to the United States today than was Vietnam in 1967. As *Washington Post* columnist Richard Cohen wrote, "where Iraq is really different from Vietnam" is that "there can be no premature, chaotic and shameful withdrawal. In the end, Vietnam didn't matter. Iraq does."[2] In November 2005, the influential senator John McCain of Arizona echoed this view, calling for ten thousand more troops to go to Iraq, arguing that the "stakes are higher" in Iraq "than they were in Vietnam."[3]

The supporters of "regime change" in Iraq made immense claims about changes not only in Iraq, but throughout the whole of the Middle East. In Iraq, the United States faces not just the prospect of retreat from those aims, but a serious reversal. The consequences of a defeat in Iraq are therefore far more significant. Politicians and planners in Washington know that their ability to intervene in other countries will be severely hampered if the United States is forced from Iraq without having achieved at least its main imperial objectives. This explains, in part, the commitment of the Democratic Party to "winning" the war in Iraq, a position that ties it in knots and leaves it incapable of leading any antiwar opposition.

We cannot rule out that the United States will crush Iraq, and will occupy the country for years to come, in order to achieve at the very least an appearance of victory. The war in Iraq will most likely end, though, as the war in Vietnam did, with a defeat of the United States. Either way, as with the Vietnam War, the highest price will be paid, and for years to come, by the occupied population, the Iraqi people, who have already suffered years of a dictatorship backed by the United States and years of war and sanctions.

Vietnam today still suffers the tragic consequences of U.S. intervention, for which no politician in Washington has ever assumed meaningful responsibility. To this day, people are suffering from the toxic chemical assault on the country. The United States dropped more than ten million gallons of Agent Orange and other defoliants containing deadly toxins.[4] But Washington has long denied responsibility for these war crimes. As Andrew Metz of *Newsday* notes, "U.S. officials have long said the Vietnamese allegations of extreme health problems are unsubstantiated and exaggerated. The government has opposed . . . [a] class action suit, which covers as many as four million alleged victims, insisting that it would invite former enemies into American courts." In March 2005, a Brooklyn federal judge dismissed charges that companies that produced chemical weapons used in Vietnam "violated international conventions on chemical warfare and ruled that the firms were shielded from liability anyway because they were contractors following military orders." The U.S. companies responsible for the devastation also have refused to accept any responsibility. Scot Wheeler, a spokesman for Dow, the major manufacturer of dioxin, put the matter succinctly: "War damages people, lives and the environment," so Dow can't be held responsible for producing weapons of war.[5]

In urging the Brooklyn judge to dismiss the lawsuit against Dow and other companies, the Justice Department made clear its real objection: "The implications of [the] plaintiffs' claims are astounding, as they would open the courthouse doors of the American legal system for former enemy nationals and soldiers claiming to have been harmed by the United States Armed Forces." In addition, the Justice Department argued that recognition of the rights of Vietnamese who suffered from dioxin poisoning would pose "a dangerous threat to the president's power to wage war."[6]

In keeping with this logic, the Justice Department has sought to challenge restrictions on the right of the U.S. military to use torture or to conduct "extraordinary renditions" of anyone it deems an "enemy" or "unlawful combatant." In the view of many in the Bush administration, the president and the executive branch are above all international law, and can conduct wars with only the most cursory congressional, judicial, or international legal oversight.[7] Indeed, in February 2002, the Bush administration formally concluded that the Geneva Conventions do not apply to U.S. actions in the "war on terror."[8] The horrors of Camp X-Ray and Camp Delta in Guantánamo, of Abu Ghraib and other U.S. prison camps in Iraq and Afghanistan, and of the outsourcing of torture to states known for their abuse of prisoners and detainees are all the logical outcome of this doctrine of impunity.

Other countries around the world now echo this same logic. Politicians who are accused of human rights abuses openly protest that they are merely protecting themselves against terrorism, like the United States, when they assassinate Palestinians, Chechens, or domestic dissidents. And, befriending Washington, a number of governments have signed on to be members of the "coalition of the willing," providing support for the United States and hoping for economic and political rewards, including potential future oil concessions in Iraq. While it was easy to mock the list of members of the coalition, the United Kingdom, Australia, Spain, Italy, and a long list of countries sent troops in numbers sufficient to allow the Bush administration to use the pretext that it was "enforcing the international will" and acting to implement United Nations resolutions in its invasion of Iraq.

Of the more than one hundred and seventy-five thousand troops in Iraq at the end of 2005, some twenty-five thousand were from outside the United States. Though the numbers have been largely kept secret, roughly twenty thousand private security guards—mercenaries—were also in Iraq, double the second-largest national contingent, the United Kingdom's.[9] These mercenaries, among them people involved in torture at Abu Ghraib, have operated in a gray area, largely outside international law.[10]

The countries that have supported the U.S. adventure in Iraq also bear responsibility for this war.

The invasion of Iraq in March 2003 and the subsequent occupation of the country have already had profound consequences for world politics, and will do so for years to come. The United States has made the world a more dangerous place, has fueled reactionary

TABLE 1[11]

COUNTRIES CURRENTLY IN IRAQ

COUNTRY	NUMBER OF TROOPS
United Kingdom	8,500
South Korea	3,200
Italy	2,600
Poland	1,500
Australia	900
Georgia	898
Romania	863
Japan	600
Denmark	530
El Salvador	380
Azerbaijan	150
Fiji	150
Latvia	135
Albania	120
Mongolia	120
Lithuania	110
Slovakia	104
Czech Republic	102
Armenia	46
Bosnia & Herzegovina	36
Estonia	34
Macedonia	32
Kazakhstan	27
TOTAL	21,137

COUNTRIES THAT HAVE WITHDRAWN TROOPS

COUNTRY	DATE OF WITHDRAWAL
Bulgaria	December 2005
Dominican Republic	May 2004
Honduras	May 2004
Hungary	December 2004
Moldova	February 2005
The Netherlands	April 2005
New Zealand	September 2004
Nicaragua	February 2004
Norway	November 2005
Philippines	July 2004
Portugal	February 2005
Spain	April 2004
Thailand	August 2004
Tonga	December 2004
Ukraine	December 2005

political currents in Iraq and beyond, has increased the likelihood of terrorist attacks at home and in the countries of visible U.S. allies, and has undermined the potential for democratic developments in the Middle East—contrary to all the claims of President Bush and his apologists.

In Iraq, the United States and its allies have run up against the limits of empire. Those responsible for this war may at some point seek to cut their losses, but it is incumbent on popular forces in the United States, in the rank and file of the U.S. military, and internationally to force the U.S. government to this conclusion at the soonest possible moment, before the consequences become far worse. We must also confront a much larger challenge: the need to transform the irrational economic and political system that led to the wars in Vietnam and Iraq and that is today very directly threatening the survival of the human species.

1.

A WAR OF CHOICE

EVERY SINGLE ARGUMENT the Bush administration made to justify the invasion of Iraq has turned out to be false. Iraq had no weapons of mass destruction, posed no imminent threat to the United States, and had no connection to al-Qaeda or to the terrorist attacks of September 11, 2001. Iraq was attacked not because it had weapons of mass destruction, but because it did not (a fact that has not been lost on other potential targets of U.S. intervention). U.S. soldiers were not greeted as liberators, and the occupation has not paid for itself, or required few troops, or been quickly concluded. Nor has the occupation made the world safer or reduced the threat of weapons of mass destruction. Indeed, it has made Iraq, the Middle East, and the world far more dangerous.

None of these facts should be a surprise. They were all publicly predicted by the antiwar movement, which the media systematically ignored. On every substantive point, the antiwar movement has turned out to have been right in its analysis, and the Bush administration has turned out to be wrong.

The collapse of the Bush administration's case for war has been so complete that the establishment media have had to retrospectively question their overly credulous coverage of the administration's claims about the war. On May 26, 2004, more than a year after the invasion of Iraq, the *New York Times* ran an article from the editors titled "The *Times* and Iraq," which noted, "We have found a number of instances of coverage that was not as rigorous as it should have been. In some cases, information that was controversial then, and seems questionable now, was insufficiently qualified or allowed to stand unchallenged. Looking back, we wish we had been more aggressive in re-examining the claims as new evidence emerged—or failed to emerge."[1] Unlike the many front-page stories, with banner headlines, warning about Iraq's weapons of mass destruction, the note was buried on page ten and did not single out any *New York Times* reporters for criticism. Most notably the article makes no mention of *Times* reporter Judith Miller, who had become a bullhorn for prowar propaganda fed to her by the Bush administration and Iraqi exiles.[2]

The *Washington Post* similarly concluded, with numerous qualifications, that its coverage "in hindsight looks strikingly one-sided at times."[3]

> "The paper was not front-paging stuff," said Pentagon correspondent Thomas Ricks. "Administration assertions were on the front page. Things that challenged the administration were on A18 on Sunday or A24 on Monday. There was an attitude among editors: Look, we're going to war, why do we even worry about all this contrary stuff?" . . .
>
> Across the country, "the voices raising questions about the war were lonely ones," [executive editor Leonard] Downie [Jr.] said. "We didn't pay enough attention to the minority."[4]

Former *Washington Post* assistant managing editor Karen DeYoung put the matter the most succinctly: "We are inevitably the mouthpiece for whatever administration is in power."[5]

Almost without exception, the explanations for the enormous gap between Bush administration rhetoric and the reality on the ground in Iraq have rested on a shared and utterly baseless assumption: that President Bush acted in "good faith," or perhaps with "an excess of idealism," in the pursuit of the objectives he announced to the world.[6] The White House may have erred by using "bad intelligence" in planning the war, or may have been duped by Iraqi exiles who wanted to trick the United States into mounting an invasion, but it acted with noble intentions.

The reality, however, is that the administration consistently manipulated intelligence to engineer popular support for a "war of choice," to use the expression of one of its main supporters, *New York Times* columnist Thomas Friedman.[7] The neoconservatives at the heart of the Bush strategy to invade Iraq even set up the Office of Special Plans at the Pentagon specifically to circumvent the State Department and Central Intelligence Agency.[8]

Bush and his top aides were determined to invade Iraq for reasons they concealed, knowing they could rely on a pliable media that would not seriously challenge the case for war but would "front-page" their claims and a Democratic Party that would crumble under the threat of appearing unpatriotic or weak on "homeland security." The White House used the Iraqi exiles not only to build the propaganda campaign for the war but in the hope they would become part of a new government in Iraq dependent on U.S. power for survival and therefore properly subservient to U.S. interests, a model with a long colonial pedigree.

The attacks of September 11, 2001, provided the pretext the Bush administration needed to portray an offensive war to reshape the Middle East as a defensive measure to protect the people of the United States. The Bush administration saw the horrific events of September 11 as an opportunity to carry out plans that long predated the attacks, and immediately set to work to target Iraq, despite the fact that the country had no link at all to the hijackings.

Indeed, leading members of the Bush administration were open about describing the post–September 11 moment as an "opportunity." After September 11, Condoleezza Rice, Bush's national security adviser and later secretary of state, asked senior national security staff to think about how to "capitalize on these opportunities," which were "shifting the tectonic plates in international politics" to U.S. advantage. "I really think this period is analogous to 1945 to 1947," she told Nicholas Lemann of the *New Yorker*. "And it's important to try to seize on that and position American interests and institutions and all of that before they harden again." [9]

Bush invoked al-Qaeda and the World Trade Center and Pentagon attacks repeatedly in his public speeches on Iraq, as the administration consciously set about selling the war to a skeptical public audience, eventually creating the false impression among a majority of the population that Iraq was connected to September 11. [10]

But the invasion of Iraq was not about terrorism, al-Qaeda, or September 11. It was about oil, an essential component of the world capitalist system, vital for production and transport in every essential industry, including the military, and it was about maintaining the popularity and agenda of a "war president," as Bush fancied himself, and parlaying that into a second presidency for an otherwise unpopular president. [11]

Had Saddam Hussein been a brutal dictator in some less strategically located country, for example in East Africa, or if he had been willing to follow orders from the White House, as he once had during the years of his worst crimes, his regime would certainly still be in place. But after his August 1990 invasion of Kuwait, he no longer served U.S. interests and was a threat to the stability of the Middle

East. For neoconservatives close to the Bush administration, the fact that Hussein remained in power after the 1991 Gulf War fostered "a lack of awe" for the United States.[12] A number of Bush advisers felt that the standing of the United States as the "indispensable nation"—a phrase coined by President Bill Clinton and echoed often by Madeleine Albright, his United Nations ambassador and secretary of state—depended on creating a stable regime in Iraq.[13] Others envisioned that "regime change" in Iraq could begin a process of "rollback" in the Middle East, serving as a springboard for further changes in the region that would ensure U.S. hegemony. "By this way of thinking, the road to Damascus, Tehran, Riyadh and Jerusalem goes through Baghdad," George Packer wrote in the *New York Times Magazine,* in "a new domino theory."[14]

At first, members of both the Clinton and Bush administrations sought to achieve "regime change" in Iraq by supporting an internal revolt, hoping for a more palatable Hussein-like figure to emerge from within the ranks of the military and the Baath Party. When that strategy failed, U.S. planners increasingly turned to a model of regime change through outside intervention.

Washington wanted a subservient regime in Iraq for a simple reason: Iraq has approximately one hundred and twelve billion barrels of proven oil reserves (only surpassed by Saudi Arabia) and oil of high quality that is relatively easy and cheap to extract. As the *Financial Times* explains, "Unlike the [oil of the] Caspian region—the 'great new frontier' of the 1990s—Iraq's crude oil is easier to access and to export. Iraq has the added advantage of being able to transport much of its output through the Mediterranean via a pipeline to Turkey—a flexibility other Middle East producers lack."[15] Iraq also sits in a region with large, increasingly important natural gas reserves.[16]

For decades, Washington has been committed to ensuring that it alone can use oil as a weapon against other countries, particularly economic and political rivals in Asia and Europe, by controlling the supply and flow of oil.[17] This objective has only grown in importance in recent years as leading economic and political competitors have become more dependent on importing Middle Eastern energy resources and as global oil reserves have declined, making it a much more expensive commodity and greatly increasing competition over access to supplies. Japan currently imports more than 85 percent of its oil from the Middle East; the United States imports only 13 percent from the region.[18] China and India also project rapidly increased energy imports in the near term, as their economic growth rates push them into greater competition with the United States.[19]

As political scientist Michael Klare rightly noted at the time of the March 2003 invasion, "The removal of Saddam Hussein and his replacement by someone beholden to the United States is a key part of a broader United States strategy aimed at assuring permanent American global dominance" in the Middle East.[20] The United States, he writes, has extended the Carter Doctrine—that the United States will defend its "vital" interest in Persian Gulf oil "by any means necessary, including military force"—to the global stage:

> Today, the Carter Doctrine stretches far beyond the Persian Gulf. It is the blueprint for the extension of U.S. military power to the world's other oil-producing regions. Just as existing U.S. policy calls for the use of military force to protect the flow of oil from the Persian Gulf, an extended Carter Doctrine now justifies similar action in the Caspian Sea region, Latin America, and the west coast of Africa. Slowly but surely, the U.S. military is being converted into a global oil-protection service.[21]

"George W. Bush's Iraq War, while duplicitous in many respects," Klare adds,

> is actually the culmination of twenty-five years of U.S. policy to ensure continued domination of the Persian Gulf and its prolific oil fields. In fact, it was a natural expression of the Carter Doctrine. . . . Seen in this light, Bush Jr. was merely applying the doctrine when he invaded Iraq in 2003.
>
> He's not the first. President Reagan cited it to justify U.S. intervention in the Iran-Iraq War of 1980–1988 to help ensure the defeat of Iran. President Bush Sr. invoked it to authorize military action against Iraq in 1991, during the first Gulf War. And Bill Clinton, though not explicitly citing the doctrine, adhered to its tenets.
>
> So the use of force to ensure U.S. access to Persian Gulf oil is not a Bush II policy or a Republican policy, but a bipartisan, American policy.[22]

Control of Iraqi oil gives the United States tremendous leverage and influence vis-à-vis competing economic and political powers that are dependent on Middle Eastern energy resources. "The reemergence of Iraq will be of historic significance," observed energy analyst Daniel Yergin, "because of the scale of the resources and because of the realignment it may portend among the major oil exporters."[23]

In their more candid moments, Bush administration apologists have acknowledged that U.S. interests in Iraq are about straight power politics. "An American-led overthrow of Saddam Hussein—and the replacement of the radical Baathist dictatorship with a new government more closely aligned with the United States," asserted former Bush speechwriter David Frum, "would put America more wholly in charge of the region than any power since the Ottomans, or maybe even the Romans."[24]

U.S. planning for the invasion of Iraq, which was otherwise so haphazard, laid out in considerable detail the "quick takeover of the country's oil fields."[25] Indeed, the first areas seized by the invading troops in southern Iraq were named Forward Operating Base Exxon and Forward Operating Base Shell.[26] Iraqis were also quick to note that in the chaos following the invasion, U.S. troops secured the interior and oil ministries, but stood by while museums, weapons caches, and even sites with nuclear-related materials were looted.[27]

Yet another rationale for the war advanced by the Bush administration centered on human rights abuses by the Iraqi regime. Saddam Hussein "used chemical weapons on his own people," President Bush declared in his State of the Union address motivating the invasion of Iraq.[28] True, if we set aside the objection that the Kurds are hardly Hussein's "own people." But we can learn how much this atrocity really concerned the political establishment by examining the history of U.S. actions in its immediate aftermath. Take, for instance, the most commonly cited example of an Iraqi chemical attack, the massacre of some five thousand Kurds in Halabja in March 1988. The brutal attack, part of a much broader government campaign of ethnic cleansing, was repeatedly referenced in 2002 and 2003 as a pretext for invading Iraq, but when the story broke in March 1988 the Reagan administration preferred to downplay or discredit it. Some in Washington encouraged the idea that Iran had actually carried out the attacks.[29]

"The issue is extremely sensitive because the Reagan Administration has moved closer to Iraq in recent years," the *New York Times* explained.[30] "Iraq, which has the second-largest oil reserves in the world after Saudi Arabia, is an important American trading partner. The United States buys an average of 447,000 barrels of Iraqi oil a day, amounting to about $2 billion a year. Last year, the United States exported $1 billion in agricultural products, including rice, wheat and meat to Iraq," the *Times* added, just six weeks before Iraq's invasion of Kuwait in August 1990, when Hussein suddenly switched from an ally to a hated enemy.[31]

When news of Halabja broke, the State Department issued a rote condemnation, but Washington continued its courtship with Iraq. "Washington's friendship for Baghdad is likely to survive one night of poison gas and sickening television film," Jim Hoagland rightly predicted in the *Washington Post* in March 1988. "TV moves on, shock succeeds shock, the day's horror becomes distant memory. The Kurds will stay on history's margins, and policy will have continuity."[32]

"Iraq has not paid much of a diplomatic price for its actions," the *Christian Science Monitor* observed at the time.[33] Indeed, on September 8, 1988, when Secretary of State George Shultz met with Saadun Hamadi, Iraq's minister of state for foreign affairs, in Washington, he expressed only "concern" about Halabja. "The approach we want to take [toward Iraq] is that, 'We want to have a good relationship with you, but that this sort of thing [the Halabja massacre] makes it very difficult,' " explained one State Department official.[34]

In fact, the U.S. government continued to provide aid to Iraq, giving the country hundreds of millions of dollars in export credit guarantees through the Agriculture Department's Commodity Credit Corporation and the Export-Import Bank. In June 1989, a delegation of U.S. businesspeople representing "twenty-three U.S. banks, oil and oil-service companies, and high-tech, construction, and defense contractors, with cumulative annual sales of $500 billion" visited Iraq and had "high-level" talks with the Baathist regime.[35] Then, on April 12, 1990, five U.S. senators "arrived in Baghdad on a trip that . . . received little notice" at the time. "The senators carried a private message from President Bush that the United States wanted to improve relations with Iraq 'notwithstanding the record of President Saddam Hussein.' " Three of the five— Bob Dole, Howard Metzenbaum, and Frank Murkowski—returned to lead the campaign to protect Iraq from U.S. sanctions for its use of chemical weapons.[36]

All of this soon changed, however, after Iraq's August 1990 invasion of Kuwait. In entering Kuwait, Iraq crossed a line, threatening the stability of the Middle East and U.S. control over its energy resources. The Halabja massacre suddenly became a source of outrage for politicians who wanted to sell the 1991 war.

Ten years later, when building the case for another war on Iraq, Bush administration officials repeatedly invoked the invasion of Kuwait and the threat Iraq posed to its neighbors, though none of Iraq's neighbors seemed to take that threat seriously at all, realizing how much an already battered Iraq would lose if it dared cross any international boundaries. Indeed, before the Bush administration kicked in its public relations campaign to "market" the war, to use the expression of White House chief of staff Andrew Card, both Condoleezza Rice and Colin Powell dismissed the idea that Iraq threatened its neighbors.[37] On February 24, 2001, Powell said that Hussein "has not developed any significant capability with respect to weapons of mass destruction. He is unable to project conventional power against his neighbors."[38] Rice, meanwhile, told CNN in July 2001, "We are able to keep arms from him. His military forces have not been rebuilt."[39]

Indeed, though it was almost never acknowledged, the United States and its junior partner, Britain, had spent thirteen years repeatedly bombing Iraq, degrading its infrastructure, before the invasion in March 2003. In clear violation of international law, British and U.S. planes sharply escalated the number of attacks on Iraq in the months before the invasion. The attacks were not conducted to protect Kurds in northern Iraq or Shias in southern Iraq, as the United States claimed, but to provoke a retaliatory strike that could provide a pretext for war and to ensure that the country would be even less able to defend itself during the planned invasion. As Michael Smith, the London *Times* journalist who obtained the "Downing Street" memos on British preparation for the invasion of Iraq, writes,

> British government figures for the number of bombs dropped on southern Iraq in 2002 show that although virtually none were used in March and April, an average of ten tons a month were dropped between May and August.
>
> But these initial "spikes of activity" didn't have the desired effect. The Iraqis didn't retaliate. They didn't provide the excuse Bush and Blair needed. So at the end of August, the allies dramatically intensified the bombing into what was effectively the initial air war.
>
> The number of bombs dropped on southern Iraq by allied aircraft shot up to 54.6 tons in September alone, with the increased rates continuing into 2003.
>
> In other words, Bush and Blair began their war not in March 2003, as everyone believed, but at the end of August 2002, six weeks before Congress approved military action against Iraq.[40]

In addition, the United States had for years flown planes and drones over Iraq, surveying every inch of its territory, further throwing into question Bush's claims about Iraq's hidden weapons of mass destruction.

By intervening in Iraq, the Bush administration hoped not only to entrench its control of the Middle East but to more firmly establish the right of the United States to intervene anywhere that it perceives as a potential threat to its imperial interests. The Bush administration, with the Democrats safely in tow, intended the war in Iraq, like its war in Afghanistan, to have a "demonstration effect," signaling to other states that the U.S. government

(i)   has the right (which on a limited basis it may extend to allies, such as Israel) to engage in "preemptive strikes" against any country it chooses;

(ii) will defer to the United Nations and other international bodies only when it suits its ends, and will dismiss them as "irrelevant" otherwise; and

(iii) will allow no challenge to the "credibility" of U.S. imperialism.

As one unnamed "hawk" quoted in the *New York Times* put it, "By setting up our military in Iraq . . . we can set an example to other countries: 'If you cooperate with terrorists or menace us in any way or even look at us cross-eyed, this could happen to you.' " [41]

2.

THE REALITY OF OCCUPATION

IN MARCH 2003, the U.S. military launched massive air strikes and mounted a ground invasion as part of a self-declared "shock and awe" campaign.[1] Iraq had already suffered eight years of war with Iran in the 1980s; the Gulf War in 1991, which badly damaged its infrastructure and left a toxic legacy of unexploded munitions and depleted uranium; and then more than twelve years of comprehensive sanctions that shattered its economy. Infant mortality rates soared during the years of sanctions, with the United Nations estimating at least five hundred thousand "excess deaths" of children under five.[2] Iraq's water supply was badly damaged, leading to numerous deaths from otherwise easily preventable waterborne diseases. Electricity was available only intermittently throughout the country, and hospitals and other essential institutions lacked vital materials, many blocked by the United States, which repeatedly exercised its veto power in the United Nations sanctions committee to cancel or hold up contracts for alleged "dual use" items (civilian goods with a potential military application). Among the banned items were lead pencils, because "carbon could be extracted from them that might be used to coat airplanes and make them invisible to radar," and materials needed for water-treatment facilities.[3]

Today, however, conditions are even worse. Three years into an occupation that its defenders boasted would rebuild Iraq, many Iraqis say conditions were better under sanctions and dictatorship. In much of the country, there is less electricity than before the invasion, with predictable consequences, including "patients who die in emergency rooms when equipment stops running."[4] Even many Iraqis who had supported the U.S. invasion, in the hope that it would bring some improvement to their lives, now denounce the occupation. "We loved the Americans when they came, I believed when they said they came to help us," said one Iraqi, Hossein Ibrahim, a former student. "But now I hate them, they are worse than Saddam."[5]

Despite the United States handing out six billion dollars in contracts to repair Iraq's electricity infrastructure, power generation is still far short of daily Iraqi needs.[6] The water supply system is in even worse shape:

> The Ministry of Municipalities and Public Works initially planned to use U.S. funds for eighty-one much-needed water and sewage treatment projects across the country, says Humam Misconi, a ministry official. That list has dwindled to thirteen. . . .
>
> Canceled projects include the $50 million project that was supposed to provide potable water to the second-largest city in the Kurdish region and a $60 million water treatment plant in Babil province, which would have served about 360,000 residents. . . .
>
> Nearly half of all Iraqi households still don't have access to clean water, and only 8 percent of the country, excluding the capital, is connected to sewage networks.[7]

One of the major corporations involved in the water disaster has been Bechtel, which signed a contract in April 2003 ensuring that "within twelve months potable water supply will be restored in all urban centers," one of many broken promises from the company.[8]

Hospitals in Iraq are in shambles. "At Baghdad's Central Teaching Hospital for Children, gallons of raw sewage wash across the floors. The drinking water is contaminated. According to doctors, 80 percent of patients leave with infections they did not have when they arrived," Jeffrey Gettleman reported in the *New York Times* in February 2004. "Iraqi doctors say the war has pushed them closer to disaster. . . . 'It's definitely worse now than before the war,' said Eman Asim, the Ministry of Health official who oversees the country's 185 public hospitals. 'Even at the height of sanctions, when things were miserable, it wasn't as bad as this.' "[9]

"Although the Iraq Ministry of Health claims its independence and has received promises of over $1 billion of U.S. funding, hospitals in Iraq continue to face ongoing medicine, equipment, and staffing shortages under the U.S.-led occupation," independent journalist Dahr Jamail, one of the few unembedded U.S. reporters in Iraq, noted in a survey of Iraqi hospitals.[10] Jamail documented the "abject failure of the U.S. to carry out even minimal humanitarian duties as occupying power."[11]

Unemployment has skyrocketed, in large part because of decisions made by the occupation authorities. After the invasion, L. Paul Bremer III, the head of the Coalition Provisional Authority in Iraq, disbanded Iraq's three hundred and fifty thousand–person army and fired thousands of state workers who were members of the Baath Party, despite the fact that party membership was required for most jobs in Iraq.[12] Roughly half of Iraqi workers are now unemployed. In June 2005, Prime Minister Ibrahim Jafari announced plans to shed even more public-sector jobs as the Iraqi government carried out the neoliberal dictates of its U.S. patrons.[13]

"Liberated" Iraqis have noted the irony that the U.S. occupation authorities and the contractors working on lucrative no-bid and cost-plus contracts don't trust Iraqis to work for them, and instead are paying millions of dollars to import foreign workers who earn many times the average Iraqi's annual income. "Every day, thousands of foreign workers drive trucks ferrying oil refining equipment and other supplies, while others cook meals and clean the laundry for . . . U.S. and foreign troops deployed in Iraq," the *Boston Globe* reported in July 2004. "Most of these jobs are filled by Americans, Koreans, Japanese, Italians, Indians, Nepalese, and other foreign workers who have been brought into the country by private contractors, according to U.S. officials. Kellogg, Brown & Root alone has thousands of foreign workers on its payroll in Iraq." [14]

"When the full history of this bloody circus is written, people will look back slack-jawed at the scale and brazenness of the occupation's corruption and incompetence," journalist Christian Parenti writes in *The Freedom: Shadows and Hallucinations in Occupied Iraq*. [15] Of the $18.4 billion Congress appropriated for "reconstruction" in Iraq, less than half has been spent and some $100 million has disappeared without any accounting, according to the *Los Angeles Times*. [16] Instead of rebuilding Iraq, money is flowing to corporate friends of the Bush administration. "More than 150 U.S. companies were awarded contracts totaling more than $50 billion, more than twice the GDP of Iraq. Halliburton has the largest, worth more than $11 billion, while thirteen other U.S. companies are earning more than $1.5 billion each," writes researcher Antonia Juhasz. "These contractors answer to the U.S. government not the Iraqi people." [17]

This principle of accountability applies to every aspect of the occupation of Iraq. Real authority rests not with Iraqis, but with occupation forces. As the Pakistani writer Tariq Ali points out in *Bush in Babylon*, we are seeing in Iraq a clear example of "imperialism in the epoch of neo-liberal economics."[18] U.S. occupation authorities passed more than one hundred regulations designed to outlive the occupation, seeking to impose a neoliberal economic straitjacket on whatever government would eventually come to power. Every aspect of Iraq's economy, other than oil, has been opened to complete foreign ownership. The Coalition Provisional Authority renewed the antiworker trade union laws of the Hussein regime and lowered taxes on business in Iraq to levels previously only dreamed about by U.S. corporations.[19]

"The Bush administration has drafted sweeping plans to remake Iraq's economy in the U.S. image," the *Wall Street Journal* reported soon after the invasion began.[20] *New York Times* economics columnist Jeff Madrick predicted that the economic plans for Iraq were likely to cause "widespread cruelty":

> By almost any mainstream economist's standard, the plan, already approved by L. Paul Bremer III, the American in charge of the Coalition Provisional Authority, is extreme—in fact, stunning. It would immediately make Iraq's economy one of the most open to trade and capital flows in the world, and put it among the lowest taxed in the world, rich or poor. . . . The new plan reduces the top personal income and corporate tax rate to only 15 percent. It reduces tariffs on imports to 5 percent. And it abolishes almost all restrictions on foreign investment. It would allow a handful of foreign banks to take over the domestic banking system.[21]

The reconstruction of Iraq has not been motivated by the needs of Iraqis but by the utopian fantasies of a handful of economic planners, explains the journalist Naomi Klein:

> A country of twenty-five million would not be rebuilt as it was before the war; it would be erased, disappeared. In its place would spring forth a gleaming showroom for laissez-faire economics, a utopia

such as the world had never seen. Every policy that liberates multinational corporations to pursue their quest for profit would be put into
place: a shrunken state, a flexible workforce, open borders, minimal
taxes, no tariffs, no ownership restrictions. The people of Iraq would,
of course, have to endure some short-term pain: assets, previously
owned by the state, would have to be given up to create new opportunities for growth and investment. Jobs would have to be lost and, as
foreign products flooded across the border, local businesses and family farms would, unfortunately, be unable to compete. But to the authors of this plan, these would be small prices to pay for the
economic boom that would surely explode once the proper conditions were in place, a boom so powerful the country would practi-
cally rebuild itself.

The fact that the boom never came and Iraq continues to tremble
under explosions of a very different sort should never be blamed
on the absence of a plan. Rather, the blame rests with the plan itself, and the extraordinarily violent ideology upon which it is
based.[22]

In addition to economic insecurity, physical insecurity for ordinary Iraqis has greatly increased. Women who formerly worked as
educators or doctors now speak of being imprisoned in their homes,
afraid to leave, and see hard-won social and political rights being
eroded.[23] Children who formerly attended school are now kept at
home by parents fearful of sending them out in public. At any moment, Iraqis know their doors may be battered down by U.S. or
British troops, with family members humiliated, arrested, and taken
off to be detained, tortured, or murdered.

Dexter Filkins of the *New York Times* opened a window into the
reality of occupation in an October 2005 profile of Lieutenant
Colonel Nathan Sassaman, an aggressive commander of the U.S.

Army Fourth Infantry Division's 1–8 Battalion. After the death of a soldier in the unit, Sassaman declared that his battalion's "new priority would be killing insurgents and punishing anyone who supported them, even people who didn't."

> The day after [Staff Sergeant Dale] Panchot was killed, Sassaman ordered his men to wrap Abu Hishma in barbed wire. American soldiers issued ID cards to all the men in the village between the ages of seventeen and sixty-five, and the soldiers put up checkpoints at the entrance to the town. Around the camp were signs threatening to shoot anyone who tried to enter or leave the town except in the approved way. The ID cards were in English only. "If you have one of these cards, you can come and go," Sassaman said, standing at the gate of the village as the Iraqis filed past. "If you don't have one of these cards, you can't."
>
> As a measure intended to persuade the Iraqis to cooperate, wrapping Abu Hishma in barbed wire was a disaster. As they lined up at the checkpoints, the Iraqis compared themselves with Palestinians, who are sometimes forced to undergo the same sort of security checks and whose humiliations are shown relentlessly on television screens across the Arab world. "It's just like a prison now," said Hajji Thamir Rabia, an old man in the village. "The Americans do night raids, come into our houses when the women are sleeping. We can't fight them. We don't have any weapons." [24]

Filkins continues:

> On a mission in January 2004, a group of Sassaman's soldiers came to the house of an Iraqi man suspected of hijacking trucks. He wasn't there, but his wife and two other women answered the door. "You have fifteen minutes to get your furniture out," First Sgt. Ghaleb Mikel said. The women wailed and shouted but ultimately complied,

dragging their bed and couch and television set out the front door. Mikel's men then fired four antitank missiles into their house, blowing it to pieces and setting it afire. The women were left holding their belongings.

"It's called the 'leave no refuge' policy," Mikel later explained to Johan Spanner, a photographer working for *The New York Times*.

That same winter in Samarra, Sassaman's men moved through a hospital and pulled a suspected insurgent from his bed. When a doctor told the Americans to leave, a soldier spat in his face. Another time, an officer told Spanner, one of Sassaman's soldiers threw a wounded man into a cell and threatened to withhold treatment unless he told them everything he knew. "We've told him he's not getting medical attention unless he starts to talk," Capt. Karl Pfuetze told Spanner.[25]

U.S. soldiers have also taken to quartering Iraqi homes and schools. "Requisitioning homes or other buildings has been widespread in Iraq for U.S. troops on missions who stay far away from bases, sometimes for several days or weeks," the Associated Press reports. "They broke into my house before Ramadan and they are still there," Dhiya Hamid al-Karbuli recounted. "We were not able to tolerate seeing them damage our house in front of our very eyes. . . . I was afraid to ask them to leave." [26]

"Marines have been making camp in seized houses," the *New York Times* reported from Husayba, the site of a major assault in November 2005, in which "fighter jets streaked overhead, dropping five hundred–pound bombs" on the town. ("At any given time, the skies over Iraq contain, in the words of one senior officer here, 'a cocktail of weapons'—from two thousand–pound bombs to one hundred–pound Hellfire missiles—waiting to be let loose should the need arise," the *Washington Post* notes.)[27]

Neither the Associated Press or the *New York Times* mentioned that quartering of troops was one of the primary complaints that the American colonists raised against King George and the British in the Declaration of Independence:

> He has affected to render the Military independent of and superior to the Civil power.
>
> He has combined with others to subject us to a jurisdiction foreign to our constitution, and unacknowledged by our laws; giving his Assent to their Acts of pretended Legislation:
>
> For Quartering large bodies of armed troops among us:
>
> For protecting them, by a mock Trial, from punishment for any Murders which they should commit on the Inhabitants of these States. . . .
>
> For depriving us in many cases, of the benefits of Trial by Jury:
>
> For transporting us beyond Seas to be tried for pretended offences.[28]

But the rights or feelings of Iraqis don't really matter in U.S. calculations. As Colonel Stephen W. Davis of the Second Marine Division, who headed the Husayba assault, explained, "We don't do a lot of hearts and minds out here because it's irrelevant."[29]

Every day, people are being harassed, killed, arrested, and tortured simply for being Iraqi. A Red Cross investigation found that the U.S. military has engaged in a "pattern of indiscriminate arrests involving destruction of property and brutal behavior towards suspects and their families" in Iraq.[30] "Sometimes they arrested all adult males present in a house," the report states, "including elderly, handicapped or sick people."[31] Of the people detained at the Abu Ghraib prison, even U.S. military intelligence officers estimated that 70 to 90 percent were arrested "by mistake."[32]

U.S. soldiers have been trained to view Iraqis, just as they were once trained to see the people of Vietnam, as less than human. They routinely call Iraqis *hajis,* the contemporary equivalent of *gooks* in Vietnam. Every Iraqi is seen as a potential terrorist, and a clear message has been given to troops from the highest levels of political and military authority: Iraqi deaths and Iraqi suffering do not matter. Indeed, Iraqis have been tortured for sport. Soldiers in the 82nd Airborne described beating Iraqis "to amuse themselves" and relieve stress. One sergeant from the division described how troops routinely "fucked" or "smoked" Iraqi PUCs—short for "Person Under Control," a term used to differentiate Iraqi detainees from prisoners of war, who have legal protections the United States does not want to recognize:

> To "Fuck a PUC" means to beat him up. We would give them blows to the head, chest, legs, and stomach, pull them down, kick dirt on them. This happened every day.
>
> To "smoke" someone is to put them in stress positions until they get muscle fatigue and pass out. That happened every day. Some days we would just get bored so we would have everyone sit in a corner and then make them get in a pyramid. This was before Abu Ghraib but just like it. We did that for amusement.[33]

These abuses began before Abu Ghraib and have continued since. Hayder Sabbar Abd, one of the many Iraqis abused at Abu Ghraib, described how "he and six other inmates were beaten, stripped naked" and "forced to pile on top of one another, to straddle one another's backs naked, to simulate oral sex" in front of onlooking U.S. soldiers. "It was humiliating," Abd recounted. "We did not think that we would survive. All of us believed we would be killed and not get out alive."[34]

Even right-wing senator Lindsey Graham of South Carolina said, "We're not just talking about giving people a humiliating experience. We're talking about rape and murder."[35]

President Bush justified the occupation of Iraq by stating that "there are no longer torture chambers or rape rooms" in Iraq.[36] But Bush oversaw the decision to reopen Abu Ghraib prison, the site of Hussein's notorious abuses and executions of political prisoners. As the investigative journalist Seymour Hersh wrote in the *New Yorker,* "The huge prison complex, by then deserted, was stripped of everything that could be removed, including doors, windows, and bricks. The coalition authorities had the floors tiled, cells cleaned and repaired, and toilets, showers, and a new medical center added. Abu Ghraib was now a U.S. military prison."[37] The United States simply announced that Abu Ghraib was under new management.

While Bush administration officials expressed outrage when pictures of torture sessions at Abu Ghraib publicly emerged, the government had already known for months about the abuses there, which had been well documented by the Red Cross and in an internal military report, and had suppressed the information. The Red Cross sent a memo to the Bush administration in February 2004 describing U.S. practices in prison camps in Iraq as "tantamount to torture" and documenting "serious violations" of Geneva Conventions governing treatment of prisoners of war.[38] "We were dealing here with a broad pattern, not individual acts," said Pierre Krähenbühl, the Red Cross director of operations. "There was a pattern and a system."[39]

U.S. Army Major General Antonio Taguba also wrote a fifty-three-page report in February 2004 describing "sadistic, blatant, and wanton criminal abuses" in U.S. detention centers.[40] But General Richard Myers, the chairman of the Joint Chiefs of Staff, admitted that he had not even read it.[41] Once word of Taguba's findings finally started to get out, White House officials pressured the news media not to release the information. CBS News held the Abu Ghraib story for two weeks, before finally running it to avoid being scooped by the *New Yorker*.[42]

The Abu Ghraib torture sessions are not isolated events, but are part of a broader pattern of torture and abuse sanctioned at the highest levels of the U.S. government. In a series of unclassified presidential orders, Justice Department rulings, and intelligence directives, intelligence and military officers have been given obscene powers to detain people secretly without any access to lawyers, with no due process, using secret evidence that is not made available to the accused; to use techniques that the United States officially considers to be torture when used by other countries; to move people to countries such as Egypt, Jordan, Morocco, and Syria, where the U.S. government knows they will be tortured; to operate with minimal supervision by legal or human rights groups; and to kill people in custody with no repercussions. As Kenneth Roth of Human Rights Watch wrote in the *Financial Times,* "Many governments torture clandestinely, but the Bush administration is the only government known to claim the power to abuse detainees as a matter of official policy." [43]

In November 2005, the *Washington Post* described a "hidden global internment network" maintained by the Central Intelligence Agency that "depends on the cooperation of foreign intelligence services, and on keeping even basic information about the system secret from the public, foreign officials and nearly all members of Congress charged with overseeing the CIA's covert actions." The "CIA interrogators in the overseas sites are permitted to use the CIA's approved 'Enhanced Interrogation Techniques,' some of which are prohibited by the U.N. convention [Against Torture and

Other Cruel, Inhuman or Degrading Treatment or Punishment] and by U.S. military law." However, "The existence and locations of the facilities—referred to as 'black sites' in classified White House, CIA, Justice Department and congressional documents—are known to only a handful of officials in the United States and, usually, only to the president and a few top intelligence officers in each host country." [44]

Indeed, at least twenty-six prisoners have died in U.S. custody in Iraq and Afghanistan, with very little accountability.[45] As a headline in the *New York Times* put it, the "C.I.A. Is Likely to Avoid Charges in Most Prisoner Deaths." [46]

Many of the methods now being used in Iraq were previously used in detention camps in Afghanistan and at Camp X-Ray and Camp Delta at Guantánamo Bay Naval Base in Cuba—and, before then, in U.S. "counterinsurgency" operations in Latin America and elsewhere. According to the *Washington Post,* people being held in the Bagram prison camp in Afghanistan

> are sometimes kept standing or kneeling for hours, in black hoods or spray-painted goggles. . . . At times they are held in awkward, painful positions and deprived of sleep with a twenty-four-hour bombardment of lights—subject to what are known as "stress and duress" techniques . . . [in a] brass-knuckled quest for information, often in concert with allies of dubious human rights reputation, in which the traditional lines between right and wrong, legal and inhumane, are evolving and blurred.
>
> While the U.S. government publicly denounces the use of torture, each of the current national security officials interviewed for this article defended the use of violence against captives as just and necessary. . . .
>
> "If you don't violate someone's human rights some of the time, you probably aren't doing your job," said one official who has super-

vised the capture and transfer of accused terrorists. "I don't think we want to be promoting a view of zero tolerance on this. That was the whole problem for a long time with the CIA." [47]

The *Post* cites the testimony at a joint hearing of the House and Senate intelligence committees by Cofer Black, then head of the CIA Counterterrorist Center, who defended the CIA's new forms of "operational flexibility" in dealing with suspected terrorists. "This is a very highly classified area, but I have to say that all you need to know: There was a before 9/11, and there was an after 9/11," Black said. "After 9/11 the gloves come off." Another official explained, "We don't kick the [expletive] out of them. We send them to other countries so they can kick the [expletive] out of them." [48]

Indeed, Bush's lawyers "advise[d] government officials that if they are contemplating procedures that may put them in violation of American statutes that prohibit torture, degrading treatment or the Geneva Conventions, they will not be responsible if it can be argued that the detainees are formally in the custody of another country." [49]

The *Wall Street Journal* reports that trainees at the U.S. Army interrogation school in Fort Huachuca, Arizona, are taught "to prey on a prisoner's ethnic stereotypes, sexual urges and religious prejudices, his fear for his family's safety, or his resentment of his fellows," techniques that were clearly used in Abu Ghraib and other Iraqi prisons. [50] Interrogation instructor John Giersdorf boasted to students that his job "is just a hair's breadth away from being an illegal specialty under the Geneva Convention." [51]

The chief of interrogations and prisons in Iraq at the time of the Abu Ghraib scandal was Major General Geoffrey Miller, who was formerly in charge of the brutal detention camp at the U.S. naval base in Guantánamo Bay, where more than seven hundred people have been in "a legal black hole" for more than four years, without any formal charges being brought against them.[52] As *New York Times* columnist Bob Herbert writes, "The Bush administration has turned Guantánamo into a place that is devoid of due process and the rule of law. It's a place where human beings can be imprisoned for life without being charged or tried, without ever seeing a lawyer, and without having their cases reviewed by a court."[53] More than twenty Guantánamo detainees attempted suicide in the space of eight days in 2003, ten in one day alone.[54]

The Abu Ghraib revelations did not end the use of torture in Iraq. A Human Rights Watch investigation released in September 2005 documented widespread prisoner abuse, "often under orders or with the approval of superior officers."[55] Occupation authorities are still holding nearly fifteen thousand Iraqis, by official counts, with perhaps many more being held off the books.[56]

Torture is just one symptom of an occupation that constantly shows contempt for the people it claims to have liberated. U.S. forces have engaged in numerous prohibited forms of collective punishment against the Iraqi population. When U.S. forces entered Falluja in November 2004, after another major assault on the city in April, their first target was Falluja General Hospital. "Patients and hospital employees were rushed out of rooms by armed soldiers and ordered to sit or lie on the floor while troops tied their hands behind their backs," the *New York Times* reported.[57] U.S. forces "considered [the hospital] a refuge for insurgents and a center of propaganda against allied forces," and said they had to target the hospital because it was releasing "what they contend are inflated civilian casualty figures."[58]

The seizure of Falluja General Hospital, a protected medical facility, was only one of many war crimes during the November assault. U.S. forces also prevented hundreds of people from leaving Falluja, forcibly returning them to a battle zone and exposing them to grave danger. "Because the United States has refused to take part in the International Criminal Court," the *New York Times* noted in reporting the incident, "it is unclear whether American troops could be held accountable." [59] None were.

"Fuck Iraq and every Iraqi in it!" a soldier scrawled on a mirror in one of the homes U.S. troops raided during the November assault on Falluja. [60] This is what liberation looks like to ordinary Iraqis.

The consequences of the occupation have been devastating. An October 2004 study by *The Lancet,* Britain's leading medical journal, estimated ninety-eight thousand "excess deaths" in Iraq in the aftermath of the U.S. invasion. [61] The figure is actually conservative, as it excludes deaths in the "mortality cluster of Falluja," the site of some of the deadliest U.S. military attacks. According to the survey, "The risk of death from violence in the period after the invasion was fifty-eight times higher . . . than in the period before the war." [62]

A study by Iraq Body Count, based only on corroborated media reports, estimated that 9,270 Iraqi civilians had been killed by direct U.S. fire in the first two years after the invasion. [63] Again, the figure is surely an understatement, since many Iraqi deaths go unreported in the media. And, as the *Columbia Journalism Review* reported in spring 2005, "If the death rate has stayed the same [as *The Lancet* survey projected], roughly twenty-five thousand more Iraqis have died." [64]

Under these conditions, it is no surprise that strong majorities of Iraqis view the U.S. troops not as liberators but as occupiers. By 2004, a survey conducted by *USA Today,* CNN, and the Gallup Organization found that 71 percent of Iraqis considered foreign troops to be occupiers, a number that rises to 81 percent outside the autonomous Kurdish region in northern Iraq. [65] A poll released by the Independent Institute for Administration and Civil Society Studies in May 2004 found that 92 percent of Iraqis viewed foreign troops as occupiers, and 2 percent saw them as liberators.[66] In the same poll, only 7 percent of Iraqis expressed confidence in "coalition forces" led by the United States.[67]

Meanwhile, the death toll has also continued to climb for U.S. soldiers and now stands at more than two thousand. Injuries too are mounting. One in six soldiers returning from Iraq reports experiencing symptoms of post-traumatic stress disorder, leading to high rates of depression and suicide.[68]

Soldiers who came to Iraq believing they were protecting the world from Iraq's weapons of mass destruction or liberating Iraqis now find they are instead being asked to subjugate a population that does not want them there. "When I first went to Iraq, I actually believed what the government was saying, that we were searching for weapons of mass destruction, we were making the country safe for democracy and things like that," one soldier who applied for conscientious objector status explained. "But when we got there, I quickly found another story. I very quickly found that the Iraqis didn't want us there. . . . If soldiers had come into *our* country and had invaded *us* and had come into *our* homes, then I would have fought back, too."[69]

3.

THE NEW WHITE MAN'S BURDEN

MOST OF THE ARGUMENTS in support of the invasion and occupation of Iraq rest on the assumption that the United States is a benevolent power in world affairs, with unique rights and responsibilities. It is a force for democracy and civilization, motivated not by greed or power but by the greater common good.

For more than a century, and with increasing confidence, the United States has reserved the right to use economic or, if necessary, military coercion to achieve what it frequently calls "stability," a euphemism for a state of affairs favorable to U.S.-based corporations, which must have a global market for their products and also a global market of labor and resources to exploit. In the words of one of its intellectual defenders, the United States is a "benevolent hegemon," intervening when or where no other power or group of powers can do so, even if, because of "anti-Americanism," many people fail to see the benefits of such actions.[1]

But as the historian Sidney Lens notes in his indispensable book *The Forging of the American Empire,* the idea of the United States as a benevolent hegemon is not new:

> The United States, like other nations, has formulated a myth of morality to assuage its conscience and sustain its image. The United States, we are told, has always tried to avoid war; when it has been

forced to take the military road, it has seldom done so for motives of gain or glory. On the contrary, the wars are fought only for such high principles as freedom of the seas, the right of self-determination, and to halt aggression. In thought, as in deed, the United States—so the myth goes—has been antiwar, anti-imperialist, anti-colonialist. It has not sought an inch of anyone else's territory, and the few colonies it acquired were treated with kindness and liberated as quickly as circumstances permitted. . . .

By and large, according to the myth, the United States has religiously respected the rights of other peoples to determine their own destiny: it has always been sympathetic to revolutionaries fighting for genuine independence; it has always refrained from interfering in the internal affairs of other nations, large or small, powerful or weak. More than any other great nation it has been guided by a selfless concern for those less fortunate.[2]

Anyone who has studied the language the Bush administration has used to justify its wars in Afghanistan and Iraq, or to explain the open-ended "war on terror" it launched in September 2001, will recognize the myth that Lens describes. In a graduation speech at West Point in June 2002, for example, President Bush said, "America has no empire to extend or utopia to establish. We wish for others only what we wish for ourselves."[3] In November 2002, he returned to this theme, asserting that the United States has "no territorial ambitions. We don't seek an empire. Our nation is committed to freedom, for ourselves and for others."[4]

As Lens argues, though,

America the benevolent . . . does not exist and has never existed. The United States has pilfered large territories from helpless or near-helpless peoples; it has forced its will on scores of nations, against their wishes and against their interests; it has violated hundreds of treaties and understandings; it has committed war crimes as shocking as most; it has wielded a military stick and a dollar carrot to forge an imperialist empire such as man has never known before; it has intervened ruthlessly in the life of dozens of nations to prevent them from choosing the leaders they did want or overthrowing, by revolution, the ones they didn't.[5]

Politicians in the United States, as well as the establishment media, have almost universally presented military interventions as defensive in nature:

> Every act of aggrandizement in the American chronicle has been valiantly camouflaged in the rhetoric of defense. . . . The innumerable wars against the Indians were a "defense" against their rampages and violations of treaties. The war against Mexico was a "defense" of Texas and a necessary measure, in the words of Secretary of State James Buchanan, "to hold and civilize Mexico." The Spanish-American War was fought to avenge the sinking of the *Maine*. . . . In Korea and Vietnam the United States, according to Harry Truman and Lyndon Johnson, was "defending" helpless small powers against Communist aggression.[6]

"The myth of morality," Lens writes, "wears thin against the aggregate of history. . . . Even a cursory look suggests that American policy has been motivated not by lofty regard for the needs of other peoples but by America's own desire for land, commerce, markets, spheres of influence, investments. . . . The primary focus has not been moral, but imperial."[7]

Though the word *imperialism* has been effectively banished from the political discourse of the left, largely because of the internalization of McCarthyism by its dominant liberal voices, the term has recently been revived—by its defenders, not its critics. For instance, the

British historian Niall Ferguson argues in his book *Empire* that the United States must "overcome its anti-imperialism and accept the responsibilities that the end of the Cold War has thrust upon it." [8]

Indeed, a number of writers and theorists have argued that imperialism—and even colonialism—must be reinterpreted in a more positive light in the aftermath of the attacks of September 11, 2001. Edward Rothstein, writing in the *New York Times* on September 7, 2002, notes that the word *imperialism*

> still jangles with jingoistic echoes. And American neo-imperialism may yet turn tragic with frustrations, as [Rudyard] Kipling long ago predicted in his misunderstood paean to "the White Man's burden." [9]
>
> Yet this idea is bound to change character. After all, instead of exploitation, imperialism is now being associated with democratic reform, sometimes to the great satisfaction of its subjects. Maybe even nineteenth-century imperialism will be reinterpreted and invoked by example since many non-Western nations developed democratic institutions solely because of imperialist influence. Imperialism's exploitation often had a virtuous flip side. [10]

Rothstein distills perfectly the logic of the white man's burden in its historical and contemporary form. Never mind the millions subjugated, killed, starved, driven into forced labor, exposed to disease, abused, denied their cultural heritage, exploited, robbed—imperialism was a force for democracy and civilization. It brought "backward" people into the light of civilization. [11]

Empire, it seems, has been given a bad rap. Max Boot, the former editor of the *Wall Street Journal* editorial page, says the world today needs the United States to provide "the sort of enlightened foreign administration once provided by self-confident Englishmen in jodhpurs and pith helmets." [12] Ferguson, who describes himself as "a fully paid-up member of the neoimperialist gang," meanwhile complains that "the British Empire has had a pretty lousy press." [13]

Another influential exponent of the neoimperialist school of thought is Michael Ignatieff, the head of the Carr Center for Human Rights Policy at Harvard University's John F. Kennedy School of Government, who gives a liberal veneer to the rather crude arguments of Boot and Ferguson. "Imperialism used to be the white man's burden," Ignatieff wrote in the *New York Times Magazine,* where he is a contributing writer, on July 28, 2002. "This gave it a bad reputation. But imperialism doesn't stop being necessary just because it becomes politically incorrect. Nations sometimes fail, and when they do, only outside help—imperial power—can get them back on their feet." [14] With Ignatieff's light touch, the brutal history of imperialism is reduced to "political correctness," not worth a moment's thought.

In another defense of empire in the *New York Times Magazine,* Ignatieff explained to readers that

> being an imperial power, however, is more than being the most powerful nation or just the most hated one. It means enforcing such order as there is in the world and doing so in the American interest. It means laying down the rules America wants (on everything from markets to weapons of mass destruction) while exempting itself from other rules (the Kyoto Protocol on climate change and the International Criminal Court) that go against its interest. It also means carrying out imperial functions in places America has inherited from the failed empires of the twentieth century—Ottoman, British and Soviet. In the twenty-first century, America rules alone, struggling to manage the insurgent zones—Palestine and the northwest frontier of Pakistan, to name but two—that have proved to be the nemeses of empires past.
>
> America's empire is not like empires of times past, built on

colonies, conquest and the white man's burden. We are no longer in the era of the United Fruit Company, when American corporations needed the Marines to secure their investments overseas. The twenty-first century imperium is a new invention in the annals of political science, an empire lite, a global hegemony whose grace notes are free markets, human rights and democracy, enforced by the most awesome military power the world has ever known.[15]

Ignatieff's chosen métier is not poetry, but his tribute to the U.S. empire is as obsequious and as divorced from reality as was Rudyard Kipling's of 1899.

It is worth examining the parallels between Kipling's moment and our own. The rhetoric used to justify the war against the Filipino people has numerous parallels to the arguments for "pacifying" Iraq today. Indeed President Bush himself explicitly made the connection between the two occupations in a speech to the Philippines Congress, on October 18, 2003.

"Together our soldiers liberated the Philippines from colonial rule," Bush informed the assembly.

> Democracy always has skeptics. Some say the culture of the Middle East will not sustain the institutions of democracy. The same doubts were once expressed about the culture of Asia. These doubts were proven wrong nearly six decades ago, when the Republic of the Philippines became the first democratic nation in Asia. Since then, liberty has reached nearly every shore of the Western Pacific.[16]

Bush's version of history was so fantastical, though, that even the *New York Times* had to gently remind readers of some inconvenient historical facts, noting that the "analogy to the American administration of the Philippines" was somewhat problematic "given that the Philippine government did not gain full autonomy for five decades" after the U.S. withdrew its forces.[17]

Indeed, the *Times* noted, the parallel raised other uncomfortable topics, given that many of Bush's "critics have argued that the justification for invading Iraq bore a resemblance to the rationale the United States used to begin that war in 1898, citing evidence, discounted as flimsy, that the battleship *Maine* had been deliberately blown up in Cuba by Spanish forces," especially now that "Bush faces similar accusations from critics questioning whether Saddam Hussein possessed weapons that posed an urgent threat."[18]

The analogy is not exact, of course. The *Maine* did, at least, sink, even if accidentally. So the scale of the lie is not the same. But in both cases a patriotic press served as a willing mouthpiece for the administration's views. Like Bush after him, President McKinley also described his reasons for mounting an invasion in messianic terms. In an interview in 1899, he recounted:

> I went down on my knees and prayed [to] Almighty God for light and guidance more than one night. And one night . . . it came to me this way—I don't know how it was, but it came . . . that we could not leave [the Filipinos] to themselves—they were unfit for self-government—and they would soon have anarchy and misrule over there worse than Spain's was; and . . . that there was nothing left for us to do but to take them all, and to educate the Filipinos, and uplift and civilize and Christianize them, and by God's grace do the very best we could by them, as our fellow-men for whom Christ also died. And then I went to bed, and went to sleep, and slept soundly.[19]

McKinley's real motives were far more base: the United States was a rapidly expanding power, seeking to exercise greater sway over maritime commerce, foreign markets, and particularly the politics of the western hemisphere ("our little region over here," as Secretary of War Henry Stimson had called it).[20] This brought the United States into conflict with Spain, the colonial power in Cuba, Guam, and Puerto Rico, as well as the Philippines. The year 1898 marked not just a confrontation with Spain that would see the United States claim all three territories as its own, using the rhetoric of liberating people from Spanish domination, but also the annexation of Hawaii, which would eventually be integrated into the United States.

Indeed, as the historian Clifford Kuhn notes, "Far from being a model for nation building and democracy, as Bush has explicitly stated, the Philippines epitomizes an American foreign policy based on dubious premises and false promises." In the Philippines, he writes,

> American troops committed atrocities, attacked civilians, and destroyed their crops and villages.
>
> By the time the war ended in 1902 (although intermittent fighting lasted for decades), more than four thousand Americans, twenty thousand rebels and perhaps two hundred thousand civilians lay dead. And the relationship of the United States to the rest of the world had permanently changed.
>
> It was only in 1946 that the Philippines were granted independence, though the State Department's own briefing papers, distributed just this week [October 2003] to the Bush entourage, still state that "U.S. administration of the Philippines was always declared to be temporary."
>
> In the intervening years, the U.S. government has continued to support a succession of antidemocratic, repressive regimes in the Philippines.[21]

Among the critics of the U.S. occupation of the Philippines was the novelist and essayist Mark Twain, who returned from an extended period of living in Europe to become the vice president of the newly formed Anti-Imperialist League. Twain spoke out in opposition to the war against the Filipinos and penned savage essays on the conduct of the war, including the massacre of hundreds of Moros by U.S. troops in 1906.[22] Black soldiers serving in segregated military units wrote back to their local newspapers, describing the horrors they witnessed and the racism of officers toward the Filipinos as well as to the black troops.[23] An official of the Red Cross reported that "American soldiers are determined to kill every Filipino in sight," describing the "horribly mutilated Filipino bodies" he witnessed.[24]

Then, as now, intellectuals and politicians cloaked the real motivations for war in noble and idealistic rhetoric but showed contempt for the people they were allegedly freeing. The United States refused to allow the Filipinos who had defeated the Spanish in Cuba and the Philippines to take power. Using the language of self-determination, they explicitly denied it to the people of both countries, just as they are doing today in Iraq.[25]

A common refrain of the defenders of U.S. empire has been, as Bush asserted, that the United States has "no territorial ambitions." The claim is demonstrably false. The U.S. conquered not only the lands of the Native Americans, who were ethnically cleansed as the colonies expanded westward, but also land from Mexico and Cuba (where Guantánamo Bay Naval Base remains a colonial vestige of the 1898 war), as well as annexing several island possessions. In any event, the argument is beside the point. A state does not need to take over the physical territory of other nations to be an imperialist power. Unlike the earlier colonial powers it has displaced, the United

States has for the most part needed only temporary occupations to achieve its aims, preferring to rule via local proxies rather than directly having to staff the governments of countries in which it has intervened to topple political leaders or crush resistance movements.

Today, the U.S. government has no interest in making Iraq the fifty-first state. But it has every interest in installing a government there that is subordinate to U.S. interests; that will ensure oil is extracted, refined, exported, and sold on terms favorable to the United States; that will provide long-term basing rights to the U.S. military in a vital region of the world; that will offer favorable terms for investment and repatriation of profits for U.S. corporations; and that can contain and, if necessary, forcibly repress nationalist or democratic movements in Iraq and in nearby states that could destabilize the Middle East.

It is rare, however, for a government to say that it is sending soldiers to kill and be killed to protect profits or the control of oil. While internal planning documents, when they are eventually declassified or are leaked, often reveal a glimpse into the real motives of elite planning, governments publicly describe their actions as defense against hostile enemies, protection of cherished values, and the spread of civilization. Such claims of civilizing foreign peoples are not merely deceptive, however. They are racist.

In discussions of Arabs and Muslims in Iraq today, for example, it is taken for granted that there is such a thing as "the Arab mind," which we must somehow learn to influence, though its workings are generally said to be all but impossible to fathom. This "Arab mind," commentators sagely observe, is particularly susceptible to "anti-Americanism," presumably because it cannot grasp all that "we" are doing to support Arab and Muslim people or because we have not found the right way to communicate our benevolence to them. This is because, we are told, Muslims reject modernity and have no conception of democracy, preferring strong men to lead them or caring only about the needs of their own "tribe."

Such ideas would be comical if they did not have such appalling consequences when applied in the real world. In describing the development of the torture policy at Abu Ghraib, Seymour Hersh writes,

> One book that was frequently cited was *The Arab Mind,* a study of Arab culture and psychology, first published in 1973, by Raphael Patai. . . . The Patai book, an academic told me, was "the bible of the neocons on Arab behavior." In their discussions, he said, two themes emerged—"one, that Arabs only understand force and, two, that the biggest weakness of Arabs is shame and humiliation." [26]

This racist logic has informed not only the torture and humiliation of Iraqis, but also the idea that Iraqis are incapable of ruling themselves and therefore need an external power to impose order, to establish institutions of governance, and to guide them: the new white man's burden.

4.

A HISTORY OF OCCUPATION

THE UNITED STATES is not the first country to conquer Iraq while announcing that it has come as a liberator rather than as an occupier. Iraqis have a long history of being subjected to—and resisting—occupation, a fact that the Bush administration and their exile Iraqi allies willfully ignored when they marched on Baghdad in spring 2003, assured of a short, decisive victory.

Those who knew even a modicum about the history of Iraq predicted a fierce nationalist response against the United States and its allies. Iraqis remember not only the more recent U.S. betrayal of Iraqis who rose up against Saddam Hussein at the end of the 1991 Gulf War, whom the U.S. encouraged and then abandoned to their slaughter, and the years of sanctions and periodic U.S. and British bombing attacks. They also recall vividly the lessons of the British occupation of Iraq in the first half of the twentieth century. The parallels between the arrogance and incompetence of the British and U.S. occupations are stunning, and help explain why so many Iraqis today disbelieve the claims of their self-proclaimed modern liberators.

Modern Iraq was born out of the ashes of the collapsing Ottoman Empire, which suffered terminal defeat in the Allied victory over

Germany and Turkey in World War I. At the end of that war, Britain, France, and the United States emerged as the primary power brokers in the struggle to draw the borders of new states; to resolve issues of oppressed groups long denied self-determination, such as the Kurds and Armenians; and to determine control over valuable trade routes, military bases, economic markets, and resources in the Middle East and western Asia.

Even before the discovery of oil in Iraq, the United Kingdom considered the area vital to control of the Persian Gulf, as it was strategically located near a major route for ships traveling to India, then the so-called jewel in the crown of the British Empire. But the prospect of exploiting oil there made the country a conquest of even greater geopolitical importance. "Iraq's rich oil resources made it the primary target of contention among the Arab territories disposed of in the postwar settlement," William Stivers writes in his book *Supremacy and Oil*, describing the scramble in the Middle East at the end of the First World War.[1]

U.S. oil companies first entered the Middle East by partnering with the Turkish Petroleum Company, which was founded in 1912 "to exploit the oil wealth of Iraq" and for a period held a monopoly on Iraqi oil concessions.[2] In August 1918, British foreign secretary Lord Balfour wrote to the Imperial War Cabinet about the prospects of large oil reserves in Iraq: "I am in favor of going up as far as Mosul," which at the time was controlled by France, "before the war is over."[3]

Through a series of treaties and military maneuvers, Britain created the state of Iraq, integrating the three provinces of Mosul (which was primarily Kurdish), Baghdad (which was primarily Sunni Muslim), and Basra (which was primarily Shia Muslim); installed a monarchy; and established mandate rule over it. Iraq's territorial borders were decided by a handful of colonial administrators with only two Iraqis present. Britain kept Kuwait, which it had first set up in 1899 to gain direct control over access to shipping lanes, out of the new state.[4]

The monarch Britain imposed on Iraq in August 1921, King Faisal, was the commander of the Arab forces who had fought alongside British troops against the Turks. The British had first tried to install Faisal as the ruler of Syria, before he was forced out in July 1920. In Iraq, his role was to serve as a figurehead. "I am an instrument of British policy," Faisal acknowledged.[5]

The so-called Eastern Committee of the British Government, then headed by Lloyd George, set this out plainly in August 1918. Iraq should be ruled by an "Arab Façade."[6] In the words of Lord Curzon, the country would be "ruled and administered under British guidance and controlled by a native Mohammedan, and, as far as possible, an Arab staff."[7] The Arabs might eventually be granted independence, but not until—in the words of Sir Mark Sykes—they had "proved themselves worthy."[8] Until then, Lord Curzon explained, the "absorption" of Iraq into the British Empire should be "veiled by constitutional fictions as a protectorate, a sphere of influence, a buffer state, and so on."[9]

According to Stivers, "Until the Arabs had proved to the advanced nations that they respected the sanctity of property and contract and could operate administrative and judicial structures in a manner pleasing to the major powers, they would remain under tutelage. Independence would be theirs only if they demonstrated that they would use their political freedom in accordance with liberal norms"—or with what today we would call "neoliberal norms": opening markets to foreign exploitation, lowering taxes, and suppressing radical measures by trade unions and the political opposition.[10]

In January 1918, President Woodrow Wilson delivered his much-praised "Fourteen Points" speech to Congress, in which he ostensibly articulated the fundamental right to self-determination for all peoples. But Lord Balfour understood clearly the real intentions behind his rhetoric about democracy and self-determination: "President Wilson did not seriously mean to apply his formulation outside Europe. He meant no 'civilized' communities should remain under the heel of other 'civilized' communities"—not that "politically inarticulate peoples" should be granted self-determination.[11]

Therefore, Balfour concluded, the United States would not stand in the way of British efforts to control Iraq and other countries in the region—or beyond. Wilson himself said that the principle of self-determination did not apply to colonies whose "peoples were yet at a low stage of civilization."[12] And Robert Lansing, Wilson's secretary of state, said the policy could not possibly be applied to Africa, peopled by "savages too low in the scale of civilization to be able to reach an intelligent decision."[13] Such racism was intimately connected to the British Empire's justification of imperialism.

After British officers and troops entered Baghdad in March 1917, Lieutenant General Sir Stanley Maude, then commander in chief of British forces in Iraq, issued a proclamation stating that the British army had come not as "conquerors or enemies, but as liberators."[14] Almost the exact same words would be repeated eighty-six years later, with no sense of irony, by the new imperial proconsuls of Iraq, Jay Garner and L. Paul Bremer III.

Then, as now, however, Iraqis perceived matters quite differently, regarding the British not as liberators but as occupiers. They saw Faisal not as their representative but as a puppet serving the interests of the real power in Iraq: the British. In 1920, the occupation was forced to call in troops from England, Iran, and India to crush a popular uprising that lasted until its defeat in February 1921. Sir Arnold Wilson complained of the rebellion, "To kick a man when he is down is the most popular pastime in the East." [15] In this view, the real victims of the occupation were the British, just as Bush today portrays the United States as the victim of Iraqi aggression.

The uprising in Iraq was not isolated but was among a broader series of rebellions throughout the British Empire, which meant it was even more important to suppress it. Winston Churchill described the 1920 revolt as "only part of a general agitation against the British Empire and all it stands for." [16] A memo from Britain's India Office connected the revolt in Iraq to the Russian Revolution of 1917, which created aspirations among Iraqis and other oppressed peoples for the "abolition of European control of all sorts throughout the East." [17] In September 1920, the Communist International held a Congress of the Peoples of the East in Baku, Azerbaijan, seeking to encourage and coordinate revolutionary movements in Asia. The manifesto of the congress denounced the colonization of Mesopotamia and Britain's efforts to control "the very rich oil fields of Basra and Mosul." [18]

A further issue for England was that it was badly overextended. The chief of the Imperial General Staff warned, in a heavily italicized internal memo, *"At the present moment we have absolutely no reserves whatever . . . with which to reinforce our garrisons in any part of the world."* [19] Britain decided therefore to use its unmatched air power to try to crush anticolonial resistance in Iraq. Colonel Gerard Leachman said the only way to deal with rebellious Kurds and Muslims was to "massacre them indiscriminately." [20] The Royal Air Force Middle East Command recommended the use of chemical weapons, namely mustard gas, against "recalcitrant Arabs" as an "experiment." [21] Winston Churchill, reading the memo, wrote, "I am highly in favor of using poisonous gases against uncivilized tribes" to "induce terror." [22]

Churchill also understood that Britain had to shore up the façade of independent statehood. In October 1922, Britain and its clients in Iraq signed an agreement that recognized Iraq's "national sovereignty" while in fact ensuring that Iraq would remain firmly under British control for years to come. Faisal agreed to be "guided by the advice of His Britannic Majesty tendered through the High Commission on all important matters affecting the international and financial obligations and interests" of Britain (much as Iraqis would later submit to an elaborate system of U.S. "advisers" in Iraq).[23]

Iraq was not allowed to command its own forces. Military action had to be approved by Britain, and any joint British-Iraqi endeavors would be under British command. The British High Commissioner could require the Iraqis to impose martial law. The agreement locked in long-term military bases, transit rights, and oil concessions for the British. And it required Iraq to pay the expenses of Britain's colonial operation there.

To achieve its aims, the British developed ties to a small class of elite Iraqis who would govern the country on their behalf, and who could rule only with Britain's backing, since they had no popular legitimacy or social base. This comprador class benefited from occupation while the vast majority of Iraqis experienced deprivation and repression. It ruled at the behest of the British, who made it clear that they would bring their military might to bear if the Arab façade did not properly fulfill its role.

Britain hoped to create in Iraq what one Colonial Office memo called "A strong Arab state, friendly to the British government, breaking the chain of possibly hostile influences."[24] "What is relevant to the present purpose," another memo stated, "is the desirability of keeping within the British sphere of influence what may prove one of the most important oilfields of the future."[25] Indeed, one oil expert predicted in 1919 that "Mesopotamia stands to become one of the world's greatest oil fields." [26]

The United States was not passive in the face of these developments. By 1910, Standard Oil of New Jersey had begun serious exploration of oil in Iraq. And by 1919, U.S. oil speculators were writing about oil rights that "properly belong to American Citizens." [27] The idea that *Iraqis* might control oil under their own land was unthinkable. The only question was whether it would be Britain, France, Turkey, or the United States that would exploit the oil for their own imperial interests. In the end, the United States decided it could best enter Iraq as a junior partner of Britain, a reversal of today's so-called special relationship between the two countries. Britain needed U.S. capital, and the United States wanted Britain to assume the risks and responsibility of guaranteeing stability.

While maintaining the fiction of Iraqi independence, the British occupation only agreed to sponsor Iraq's application to the League of Nations in 1932, fifteen years after Lieutenant General Maude's deceleration. Behind the scenes, Britain secured agreements that greatly limited Iraqi sovereignty.

Resistance to British rule continued through the 1920s and 1930s, breaking out in periodic rebellions, but World War II created a new set of conditions that would be decisive for Iraq's fate. At the end of the war, the United States emerged as the preeminent global power in the Middle East, displacing Britain and France. And in 1949, India finally achieved independence from Britain, beginning a period of successful anticolonial independence struggles throughout Africa, Asia, and the Middle East that would reshape global politics.

International developments helped fuel the independence struggle in Iraq. Inspired by the example of the nationalization of Iran's oil under Mohammed Mossadegh in 1951, Iraq's competing parties started to work more collaboratively, and for the first time formed a united national liberation front. At the same time, increasing oil revenues made the Iraqi state less dependent on popular support—and strengthened the highly militarized state bureaucracy. "As the government became more rigid and repressive," notes Samira Haj, "the political opposition became more articulate and defiant."[28] The actions of the Iraqi government "forced the moderates within the opposition to lose confidence in the strategy of reforming the existing regime."[29] In July 1958, Iraqis finally achieved Iraqi independence, ending the British-installed monarchy.

"The mood . . . of revolt" that led to the revolution in 1958 "did not arise in a single event," writes Iraqi historian Hanna Batatu, "but accumulated slowly and gradually."[30] The 1958 revolution was led by the Free Officers of the Iraqi army. "The strong feelings that simmered in the depths of the people," Batatu notes, "simmered also in the depths of the army. It is not difficult to discover the reasons. The army had since 1935 rested largely on universal conscription, and tended on that account to mirror the society in all its various layers, and was bound eventually to reflect its basic passions and antagonisms. More than that . . . the bulk of the officer corps was drawn from the poor and middle classes."[31] The officers "became settled in the conviction that an irreconcilable conflict existed between the monarchy" installed by the British "and the needs of Iraq."[32] The night the Iraqi monarch, Nuri as-Said, fell, writes Batatu, "the statue of Faisal, the symbol of the monarchy, lay shattered, and the figure of General Maude, the conqueror of Baghdad, rested in the dust outside the burning old British Chancellery."[33]

The achievement of Iraqi independence relied on a wide range of opposition forces, including nationalists, Free Officers, pan-Arabists, religious factions, and members of the Iraqi Communist

Party. "The fragile unity of the opposition," however, "could not be sustained in the postrevolutionary period," and the Baath Party soon emerged as the leading force in Iraqi politics.[34] To consolidate control, the party organized a coup in 1963 and carried out a systematic campaign of slaughter of communist militants and sympathizers. In its campaign against dissidents, the Baath Party relied on lists supplied by the U.S. Central Intelligence Agency, which had supported the rise of the Baathists as a bulwark against communist revolution in Iraq.[35]

Here lie the origins of the U.S. government's longstanding support for Saddam Hussein, who rose within the ranks of the Baath Party, becoming vice president after another Baath coup in 1968 and president in 1979. The Baathists concentrated more and more power in the hands of a vast state bureaucracy and security apparatus. Any dissent led to torture, imprisonment, or execution. As the Italian journalist Ilario Salucci writes in *A People's History of Iraq*:

> The Baath Party that took power in 1968 numbered only a few hundred members, an organization desperately searching for a social base. It did not look for support among the country's poor peasants or workers; in fact, its aim from the start was to neutralize the subaltern classes. . . . It looked to build its power base among the middle-class members of the state apparatus (as well as the armed forces, which have grown out of all proportion over the years), the new middle-class strata totally dependent upon the state, and the various rural middle classes.[36]

The U.S. government continued to support Hussein during the brutal repression of his opponents, including a deadly campaign of ethnic cleansing against the Kurds in the 1980s. The United States also encouraged Hussein to attack Iran after the overthrow of Shah

Mohammad Reza Pahlavi in 1979, fearing that Iran would inspire other Islamic revolutions in the Middle East.

Washington turned against Hussein only when he acted independently by invading Kuwait in August 1990, perhaps believing he could achieve there what the United States had in Panama the year before, regime change from without and the installation of a puppet government, and possibly also thinking that the U.S. government had given tacit consent to the invasion.[37] In any event, he badly miscalculated. The U.S. war machine swung into motion and, as in 2002 and 2003, would not be deterred, even when opportunities for a negotiated Iraqi withdrawal from Kuwait were clearly available. The United States mercilessly slaughtered the retreating Iraqi army to send a message to the world: this is the price of defiance.

As the Kuwait occupation collapsed, Kurds and Shia, as well as some Sunnis in the army, rose up in an attempt to overthrow the Hussein government. President Bush had verbally encouraged the rebellion, but when it occurred, he and his advisers preferred to keep Saddam Hussein in power rather than support a revolution they did not control. As the veteran Middle East journalist Charles Glass, who was in Iraq at the time of the uprising, wrote, "The Iraqi people themselves should have been allowed to overthrow the bastard in 1991, but the United States never wanted that. When it comes to changing regimes in the Middle East, as in Latin America of old, Americans prefer not to leave it to the natives."[38]

In the post–Gulf War period, the first Bush and Clinton administrations sought to achieve a controlled changing of the guard in Iraq. Only when it became apparent that the strategy of regime change from within was not feasible did the second Bush administration decide it would seek regime change from without, armed with the cover of responding to the attacks of September 11.

Rather than being greeted as liberators, the U.S. troops now occupying Iraq are seen as conquerors. The U.S. corporate media and politicians portray Iraqis who resist occupation as Baathist remnants, "dead-enders," and al-Qaeda operatives, but they are for the most part ordinary Iraqis who know full well the history of imperial powers "bringing democracy" through bombs and bayonets. Iraqis also know the history of imperial powers using divide-and-rule tactics, as well as the threat of "civil war," to justify their presence.

Iraq today does not have a united national liberation front as it did in the 1950s, in part because of the legacy of the 1963 massacres but also because of the steady erosion of secularism under the impact of thirteen years of sanctions and external attacks. But it has a long tradition of secular nationalism and anticolonialism that means Iraqis will not quietly accept occupation by a foreign power.

5.

THE RESISTANCE IN IRAQ

BY NOW IT IS CLEAR that most Iraqis want the United States to leave. From mainstream media accounts, though, most observers could be forgiven for believing that only an isolated minority of senior Baathists, foreign fighters, and nihilists is standing up to the United States. "As if to underline their misunderstanding of the world, American military spokesmen call Iraqis who are resisting their invasion 'terrorists.' Who else on earth would call a man who fights a foreign soldier in his own country a terrorist?" the journalist Charles Glass wrote presciently only weeks after the invasion.[1]

The term *foreign fighters* is a mantra at almost every U.S. press conference on the war. It is a sign of the level to which the propaganda for this war has been internalized by the establishment media that no one blinks at such proclamations. In the standard usage, however, U.S. troops, who have traveled thousands of miles to invade and occupy Iraq, knowing in most cases not a word of Arabic or a thing about Iraqi culture or society, are not foreign fighters and are not "interfering in Iraqi affairs" (the charge repeatedly leveled by the United States against Iran, Syria, and Jordan).

"We've made clear we would oppose any outside interference in Iraq's road to democracy," White House spokesperson Ari Fleischer told reporters, without a trace of irony, in April 2003.[2] In other words, the world should stand aside and let the United States determine Iraq's future.

Before the invasion of Iraq, the United States downplayed the idea that it would face any resistance. Bush officials believed the fantasy of Iraqi exiles such as Kanan Makiya that invading troops would be welcomed "with sweets and flowers."[3] Vice President Dick Cheney told NBC, "We will, in fact, be greeted as liberators."[4] When the invasion began, the government's script seemed briefly to fit the facts on the ground. Iraq's military quickly collapsed under the impact of the U.S. attack, with the mass desertion of soldiers who understood it would be suicidal to engage in conventional warfare against the overwhelming military might of the invading armies. The media were quick to seize on images of Iraqi jubilation, particularly the carefully orchestrated television photo opportunity of U.S. soldiers toppling a statue of Saddam Hussein in Firdos Square, falsely portrayed as popular action undertaken by Iraqis themselves, with echoes of the thousands of Germans who defied the authorities to tear down the despised Berlin Wall in November 1989.[5]

But the media and the White House badly misread Iraqis' real feelings. Certainly, many were happy to see a hated dictator gone, but this did not make them pro-occupation. Iraqis were perfectly capable of hating Saddam Hussein and hating George Bush at the same time, and with equal fervor, as the slogans from anti-occupation demonstrations soon revealed. Indeed, two years after the invasion, a genuine popular toppling of Hussein's figure occurred—alongside the toppling of figures of George Bush and Tony Blair.

> Saddam Hussein's effigy was pulled down again in Baghdad's Firdos Square at the weekend. But unlike the made-for-TV event when U.S. troops first entered the Iraqi capital, the toppling of Saddam on the occupation's second anniversary was different.

Instead of being done by U.S. marines with a few dozen Iraqi by-standers, three hundred thousand Iraqis were on hand. They threw down effigies of Bush and Blair as well as the old dictator, at a rally that did not celebrate liberation but called for the immediate departure of foreign troops.[6]

In the immediate aftermath of the invasion in March 2003, Iraqis understandably felt a brief moment of hope that the future might be better now that the dreadful era of sanctions and dictatorship had ended. Few Iraqis, it seems, imagined things could get worse than they already were. It did not take long for disillusionment to sink in, however, as the occupation showed in practice its inability to provide security for ordinary Iraqis or to bring about positive change in their day-to-day lives, and as Iraqis experienced firsthand the arrogance and violence of the occupation. In Falluja, one month into the occupation, U.S. troops fired on a peaceful demonstration of Iraqis upset by troops taking over a local school, killing fifteen people and wounding sixty-five. "We won't remain quiet over this," said Ahmad Hussein, whose son was shot. "Either they leave Falluja or we will make them leave."[7]

The city of Falluja, which later would become a central target for U.S. troops, actually had a long history of opposition to Saddam Hussein, undermining the claim that resistance to the U.S. occupation was organized by Hussein and small "pockets of dead-enders," in the words of Defense Secretary Donald Rumsfeld.[8]

On May 1, 2003, Bush declared an end to "major combat operations" in a comically staged battleship speech off the coast of San Diego.[9] When the attacks on U.S. troops continued, though, and as more soldiers were killed, White House officials asserted that the insurgency was being directed by Hussein and put a twenty-five-million-dollar bounty on his head. Then when Hussein was captured in December 2003 and the insurgency continued, Bush blamed foreign interference and said the formation of a "sovereign" provisional Iraqi government would quell the unrest. After that failed, the administration said the stage-managed elections of January 2005 would bring an end to the resistance. Once again, though, the violence continued—and, in fact, increased.

In response to the escalating insurgency, the Bush administration has returned to its mantra that Iraq is the central front in its battle against al-Qaeda and that the resistance in Iraq is largely of foreign origin. But this is fiction. After collectively punishing the three hundred thousand people of Falluja and killing more than one thousand in November 2004, occupation authorities acknowledged that they had detained only seventy-two people with foreign passports.[10] In January 2005, military officials in Iraq claimed they were holding three hundred and twenty-five foreign fighters, who "could be transferred out of the country for indefinite detention elsewhere, the officials said, as they have been deemed by the Justice Department not to be entitled to protections of the Geneva Conventions."[11] Setting aside the strong possibility that many of the captured individuals were Iraqis who had foreign work or residency papers, and that many may have been innocent, this would mean less than 4 percent of all detainees in Iraq are foreign fighters.[12]

Among sober analysts of the resistance, the *Financial Times* notes, "The most important point of agreement is that, although foreign fighters allied with Abu Musab al-Zarqawi continue to gain the most attention, the insurgency remains overwhelmingly domestic, Sunni and nationalist."[13] In a detailed study for the Center for Strategic and International Studies, military analyst Anthony Cordesman found that "the insurgency seems to remain largely Iraqi and Sunni dominated," while "an overwhelming majority of those captured or killed have been Iraqi Sunnis, as well as something like 90–95 percent of those detained."[14]

Writing about "Arab and Islamist groups with significant numbers of foreign volunteers, as well as Iraqi Islamist extremists . . . like the one led by Abu Musab al-Zarqawi," Cordesman concludes, "It is unlikely that such groups make up more [than] 10 percent of the insurgent force, and probably only make up around 5 percent."[15]

Nor is the opposition exclusively Sunni in character. One of the leading voices against the occupation has been Shia cleric Moqtada al-Sadr. As historian Gareth Porter observes,

> Shiite responsiveness to al-Sadr's appeals to oppose British actions symbolizing the loss of Iraqi independence should have come as no surprise. For a year and a half, it has been clear that Moqtada al-Sadr has enjoyed widespread support among Shiites because of his anti-occupation stance. Sadr's popularity had skyrocketed in April 2004, when the Mahdi Army challenged foreign occupation troops in eight different Shiite cities, including Basra. According to an article by counterinsurgency specialists Jeffrey White and Ryan Philips in *Jane's Intelligence Review*, polling by an Iraqi research organization showed that only one percent of those surveyed had supported him in December 2003, but 68 percent supported him when his forces were fighting U.S. troops in April 2004.
>
> The stunning transformation of Basra from a secure rear area for U.S. and British troops into a center of anti-occupation agitation reveals the utter weakness of the Shiite political base on which the United States must now rely to sustain its occupation of the country.[16]

On several occasions Sunnis and Shias have taken to the streets together in defiance of the United States. In April 2004, some two hundred thousand Iraqis marched in Baghdad under unified Shia and Sunni anti-occupation banners. According to a report on the demonstration in London's *Guardian* newspaper, people chanted "Long live Moqtada, long live Falluja, long live Basra, long live Kerbala," referring to "the various cities where Shias have attacked coalition forces." [17] After the demonstration, Harith al-Dhari, an imam at the Umm al-Qura mosque in Baghdad, said, "The Americans consider themselves a safety valve against sectarian conflict, but this is an excuse for extending their stay. Here in this mosque and in this gathering we have the proof that all groups are united. We all want the coalition to leave this country." [18]

That Sunnis and Shias have come together is in no way unprecedented. Historically, most Iraqis, influenced by secular and nationalist politics, have thought of themselves as Arab or Iraqi rather than Sunni or Shia. Indeed, Shia and Sunni Iraqis have long lived and worked together and intermarried. "There are Shiites living throughout Iraq, including Kurdistan, and similarly there are Sunnis, and Christians, who have peacefully co-existed with Shiites for many centuries," explains Iraqi journalist Sami Ramadani. "There is no history of communal strife or civil war in Iraq, and the degree of socioeconomic integration and unity of purpose amongst the Iraqi people is often underestimated. There is also a powerful secular tradition in Iraq that transcends all religions and sects." [19]

The fundamental division in Iraq today is not between Sunni and Shia, or other religious or ethnic groups, argues Wamidh Nadhmi of Baghdad University, but between "the pro-occupation camp and the anti-occupation camp."

> The pro-occupation people are either completely affiliated to the United States and Britain, in effect puppets, or they saw no way to overthrow Saddam without occupation. Let's agree not to indulge in slander but discuss the issue openly. Unfortunately, the pro-occupation people tend not to distinguish between resistance and terrorism, or between anti-occupation civil society and those who use violence. They call us all Saddam remnants, reactionaries, revenge-seekers, mercenaries, misguided, or foreigners. [20]

As Nadhmi suggests, all resistance in Iraq is characterized by pro-occupation forces as terrorism, a phenomenon with a long colonial legacy. South African anti-apartheid activists in the African National Congress, Vietnamese fighting U.S. state terrorism, Algerians fighting the murderous French occupation, and Indians seeking freedom from British colonial rule have all been dismissed as terrorists. The hypocrisy runs far deeper, though. In every case, those who denounce violence most self-righteously are the military and political leaders who use preponderant military force with impunity, while simultaneously blocking meaningful avenues for peaceful opposition.

We should not be surprised that people would engage in guerrilla attacks when confronting the world's greatest military power, armed with unimaginable technological advantages. As Glenn Perusek points out, "Weak forces with local popular support have long enjoyed success with hit and run irregular guerrilla tactics against occupying enemies with overwhelming military superiority. It is precisely this force asymmetry that imposes such tactics on them." [21]

"As a consequence of its overwhelming power and prowess, the American Army is not likely to face an enemy similar to itself," Dexter Filkins of the *New York Times* observes. "It is more likely to face guerrillas. Guerrilla wars typically begin when a smaller army is confronted by a larger one, forcing it to turn to the advantages it has: its ability to hide amid the population, its knowledge of the local terrain, its ability to mount quick and surprising attacks and then melt away before the larger army can strike back. This is more or less the case in Iraq, as it was in Vietnam." [22]

Certainly in Iraq opportunistic groups and individuals have carried out indefensible acts of terrorism, including sectarian attacks completely at odds with achieving genuine national liberation for

Iraqis. But, as Ramadani points out, "Of the average of three thousand military operations per month against the occupation forces across Iraq, the terrorist operations that target civilians and grab the daily headlines are not many more than thirty per month."[23]

A small minority in Iraq has attempted to provoke a civil war between Sunnis and Shiites, Kurds, and other minorities. But Iraqis themselves have been quick to reject such sectarian attacks. In March 2005, the Muslim Scholars Association denounced a suicide bombing in Hilla that killed more than one hundred and twenty Iraqis. "This operation will open the door for our enemies to carry out more of their evil designs in Iraq," the organization said. "The association demands that all such attacks against innocent Iraqis be stopped."[24] Ahmed Abdul-Ghafur, imam of the Sunni Umm al-Qura mosque, also protested the attack in Hilla, a predominantly Shia city. "This is not the right way to drive the occupation out," he said. "Killing Iraqis is not the way to liberation. . . . We call upon those who have power over these groups to stop massacring Iraqis."[25] That same month, Iraqi oil workers and trade unionists from Basra marched in Baghdad to protest the killing of oil workers, chanting, "No, no, to terror!"[26] For the most part, though, the establishment media have largely ignored such protests by trade unionists, women's groups, and secularists opposed to the occupation.

Indeed, there is no single resistance in Iraq but a broad resistance struggle that takes a variety of forms. "The insurgency is not a monolithic or united movement directed by a leadership with a unitary and disciplined ideological vision," writes Ahmed Hashim of the United States Naval War College's strategic research department. "Its range encompasses all classes, both urban and rural. Its ranks include students, intellectuals, former soldiers, tribal youths, farmers, and Islamists."[27]

Arundhati Roy correctly argues that "it is absurd to condemn the resistance to the U.S. occupation in Iraq as being masterminded by terrorists or insurgents or supporters of Saddam Hussein." As she points out, "Like most resistance movements, it combines a motley range of assorted factions. Former Baathists, liberals, Islamists, fed-up collaborationists, communists, etc. Of course, it is riddled with opportunism, local rivalry, demagoguery and criminality. But if we are only going to support pristine movements, then no resistance will be worthy of our purity." [28]

In challenging their occupation, the people of Iraq have transformed the calculus of empire. "What if there had been no resistance in Iraq?" asks Tariq Ali. "The warmongers would have claimed that the occupation was a triumph, established a collaborationist regime and moved on to change the regime in Syria and, possibly, Iran. Dissent in the U.S. and Britain would have been neutered, the media would have remained friendly and the lies used to justify the war would have been happily forgotten. The means, we would have been told, justify the ends. And the snapshots of Iraqis being tortured would have remained a family secret." [29]

The people of Iraq have every right to resist U.S. occupation. Our main task is not to dictate to Iraqis how they should resist or to insist that people facing the most awesome military force in human history must be nonviolent but, as Arundhati Roy suggests, to "shore up our end of the resistance by forcing the U.S. government and its allies to withdraw from Iraq." [30]

6.

THE LOGIC OF WITHDRAWAL

WE FIND OURSELVES in a remarkable situation today. Despite a massive propaganda campaign in support of the occupation of Iraq, a clear majority of people in the United States now believes the invasion was not worth the consequences and should never have been undertaken. A November 2005 *Washington Post*–ABC poll found that

> Bush has never been less popular with the American people. Currently 39 percent approve of the job he is doing as president, while 60 percent disapprove of his performance in office—the highest level of disapproval ever recorded for Bush in *Post*-ABC polls. . . .
>
> Nearly six in ten—58 percent—said they have doubts about Bush's honesty, the first time in his presidency that more than half the country has questioned his personal integrity. . . .
>
> Iraq remains a significant drag on Bush's presidency, with dissatisfaction over the situation there continuing to grow and with suspicion rising over whether administration officials misled the country in the run-up to the invasion more than two years ago.
>
> Nearly two-thirds disapprove of the way Bush is handling the situation there, while barely a third approve, a new low. Six in ten now believe the United States was wrong to invade Iraq, a seven-point in-

crease in just over two months, with almost half the country saying they strongly believe it was wrong.

About three in four—73 percent—say there have been an unacceptable level of casualties in Iraq. More than half—52 percent—say the war with Iraq has not contributed to the long-term security of the United States. . . .

The war has taken a toll on the administration's credibility: A clear majority—55 percent—now says the administration deliberately misled the country in making its case for war with Iraq—a conflict that an even larger majority say is not worth the cost.[1]

Likewise, people strongly disapprove of the foreign policy of Republicans and Democrats in Congress, particularly their position on the war in Iraq.[2]

In a September 2005 *New York Times*–CBS News poll, support for immediate withdrawal stood at 52 percent, a remarkable figure when one considers that very few political organizations have articulated an "Out Now" position.[3]

The official justifications for the war have been exposed as complete fallacies. Even conservative defenders of U.S. empire now complain that the situation in Iraq is a disaster.

Yet many people who opposed this unjust invasion, who opposed the 1991 Gulf War and the sanctions on Iraq for years before that, some of whom joined mass demonstrations against the war before it began, have been persuaded that the U.S. military should now remain in Iraq for the benefit of the Iraqi people. We confront the strange situation of many people mobilizing against an unjust war but then reluctantly supporting the military occupation that flows directly from it.

In part, this position is rooted in the pessimistic conclusions many drew after the February 15, 2003, day of international demonstrations—perhaps the largest coordinated protest in human history—failed to prevent the war. This pessimism was exacerbated by some of the leading spokespeople for the antiwar movement, who misled audiences by suggesting that the demonstrations could stop the war. As inspiring as the demonstrations were, it would have taken a significantly higher degree of protest, organization, and disruption of business as usual to do so.

The lesson of February 15 is not that protest no longer works, but that protest needs to be sustained, coherent, forceful, persistent, and bold—rather than episodic and isolated. And it needs to involve large numbers of working-class people, veterans, military families, conscientious objectors, Arabs, Muslims, and other people from targeted communities, not just as passive observers but as active participants and leaders.

We will need this kind of protest to end the occupation of Iraq. But we will also need to be able to answer the objections and concerns of thoughtful, well-meaning people who have been persuaded by one or more of the arguments for why U.S. troops should remain in Iraq, at least until "stability" is restored. Below, I outline eight reasons why the United States should leave Iraq immediately, addressing common arguments for why the United States needs to "stay the course."

1. THE U.S. MILITARY HAS NO RIGHT TO BE IN IRAQ IN THE FIRST PLACE.

The Bush administration built its case for invading Iraq on a series of deceptions. The rhetoric about Iraq's weapons of mass destruction and the imminent threat Saddam Hussein posed was meant to justify the nullification of Iraq's sovereignty and to explain why the

United States did not need further United Nations authorization to invade Iraq and topple its government. The war in Iraq was sold on the idea that the United States was preempting a terrorist attack by Iraq. But Iraq posed no threat. The country was disarmed and had overwhelmingly complied with the extremely invasive weapons inspections, even after it was proved that the United States was illegally using the inspections to gather intelligence it would use in its military campaign against Iraq.[4] "I would say that we felt that in all areas we have eliminated Iraq's capabilities fundamentally," said Rolf Ekeus, the UN executive director of weapons inspection from 1991 to 1997.[5] In a rare moment of honesty, Vice President Dick Cheney told CNN in March 2001, "I don't believe [Saddam Hussein] is a significant military threat today."[6]

As the case for war has crumbled, so has the case for occupation, which also rests on the idea that the United States can violate the sovereignty of the Iraqi people and all the laws of occupation, such as the Hague and Geneva Conventions, which clearly restrict the right of occupying powers to interfere in the internal affairs of an occupied people.[7]

2. THE UNITED STATES IS NOT BRINGING DEMOCRACY TO IRAQ.

Having failed to find any weapons of mass destruction in Iraq—the first big lie of the invasion—the United States has turned to a new big lie: George Bush, Donald Rumsfeld, John Negroponte, Condoleezza Rice, John Bolton, and their friends are bringing democracy to the Iraqi people.

Democracy has nothing to do with why the United States is in Iraq. The Bush administration invaded Iraq to secure long-established imperial interests in the Middle East—the same reason Washington backed Saddam Hussein as he carried out the worst of his crimes against the Iraqi people, the Kurds, and the Iranians (crimes that were later used to justify going to war against him in 1991 and removing him from power in 2003).

The United States has recognized for decades that control over Middle Eastern energy resources is a prerequisite for U.S. global hegemony. The centrality of oil to U.S. imperial calculations has only increased since the United States first sought to replace the British and French as the outside power controlling the region's energy resources in the period after World War II. U.S. economic, military, and political competitors in Europe and Asia, particularly China and India, need to greatly increase their energy imports from the Middle East and, in fact, are proportionally far more dependent on oil from the region than is the United States, which gets most of its oil from its own reserves, as well as from Canada, Venezuela, and other sources closer to home. Thus there is increasing competition over control of oil, oil pipelines, and oil shipping routes.

As the Bush administration document *The National Security Strategy of the United States of America* clearly laid out in September 2002, the United States will not allow the emergence of any potential competitor, seeking to preserve the massive gap between itself and other powers.[8]

By invading Iraq, Washington hoped not only to install a regime more favorable to U.S. oil interests. It hoped to use Iraq as a staging ground for further interventions to redraw the map of the Middle East. Several U.S. bases have been established in Iraq and are likely to remain long after U.S. troops are expelled.[9] The largest U.S. embassy in the world today is in Baghdad.[10]

All of this has nothing to do with democracy. In fact, the United

States has long been a major obstacle to any secular, democratic, nationalist, or socialist movements in the region that stood for fundamental change, preferring instead what is euphemistically called "stability," even if it meant supporting the most reactionary fundamentalist religious forces or repressive regimes. This led it to align not only with an expansionist Israel, to defend Israeli occupation and settlement of Palestinian lands, and to allow Israel to develop nuclear weapons, but to support the overthrow of Mossadegh in Iran in 1953 and to arm and befriend the repressive regime that replaced him. Washington has historically backed—and continues to support—the royal family of Saudi Arabia. In the words of the *New York Times,* the two countries have agreed to a "basic compact: the Saudis deliver oil, the Americans deliver the weaponry that protects the oil." As one Bush official put it, "Oil runs the world and the Saudis are the linchpin of oil production."[11]

The U.S. government opposes genuine democracy in the Middle East for a simple reason: if ordinary people controlled the region's energy resources, they might be put toward local economic development and social needs, rather than going to fuel the profits of Western oil companies.

Despite all the hype about Iraqis deciding their own future, an examination of the U.S.-sponsored elections of January 2005 shows how hollow the claims of supporting democracy are in practice. The United States was forced by popular Iraqi pressure to hold elections far earlier than it had hoped, particularly given that its own hoped-for proxies, such as Ahmed Chalabi and Iyad Allawi, had so little actual support among the Iraqi people. Having succumbed to popular opinion and called an election, the occupation authorities then worked to gain control of the process and to turn events to their own advantage. Iraqis were not given actual candidate lists until the day of the vote. Meanwhile, the leading parties campaigned by raising popular slogans calling for withdrawal of occupation troops, but officially dropped this demand under U.S. pressure in the days before the election.[12]

Many Iraqis thought that by voting they would bring about an end to the occupation, but the reality was quite different.[13] As Phyllis Bennis of the Institute for Policy Studies wrote, the elections were designed "to provide a veneer of credibility and legitimacy to the continuation of U.S. control of Iraq," helping to establish a "U.S.-friendly government that will welcome the U.S. military bases in Iraq."[14]

Finally, it is important to raise a larger point. Democracy cannot be "installed" by outside powers, at gunpoint. Genuine democracy can come about only through the struggle of people for control over their own lives and circumstances, through movements that are themselves democratic in nature. When confronted with such movements, such as the 1991 Iraqi uprising, the U.S. government has consistently preferred to see them crushed than to see them succeed.

3. THE UNITED STATES IS NOT MAKING THE WORLD A SAFER PLACE BY OCCUPYING IRAQ.

The invasion of Iraq has made the world a far more unstable and dangerous place. By invading Iraq, Washington sent the message to other states that anything goes in the so-called war on terror. Though the defenders of American exceptionalism insist that such rights "are not universal," other countries will not necessarily accept this argument.[15] After September 11, India called its nuclear rival Pakistan an "epicenter of terrorism."[16] Israel has carried out "targeted assassinations" of Palestinians, bombed Syria, and threatened to strike Iran, using the same rationale that Bush did for the invasion of Iraq. "You don't negotiate with terrorism, you uproot it. This is simply the doctrine of Mr. Bush that we're following," explained Uzi Landau, Israel's minister of public security.[17]

The danger of the Iraq war precedent should not be underestimated. Dozens of countries around the world have the potential to develop weapons of mass destruction. Other countries, such as Israel, India, and Pakistan, have proven nuclear, chemical, and biological weapons capacities, with the complicity and protection of the United States.

Furthermore, the invasion of Iraq is spurring the drive for countries to develop a deterrent to U.S. power. The most likely response to the invasion of Iraq is that more countries will pursue nuclear weapons, which may be the only possible protection from attack, and will increase their spending on more conventional weapons systems. Each move in this game has a multiplier effect in a world that is already perilously close to the brink of self-annihilation through nuclear warfare or accident.

Meanwhile, the invasion has also quite predictably increased the resentment and anger that many people feel against the United States and its allies, therefore making innocent people in these countries far more vulnerable to terrorism, as we saw in the deadly attacks in Madrid on March 11, 2004, and London on July 7, 2005. Despite the denials of politicians, the two cities were targeted because of their role in the Iraq occupation, as the majority of people in both countries understood.[18]

The United States is reviled not because people "hate our freedoms," as Bush suggests, but because people hate the very real impact of U.S. policies on their lives.[19] Global opinion polls show a precipitous drop in public approval of the United States, with increasing resentment at a range of U.S. policies.[20] As the British play-wright and essayist Harold Pinter observed, "People do not forget. They do not forget the death of their fellows, they do not forget tor-ture and mutilation, they do not forget injustice, they do not forget oppression, they do not forget the terrorism of mighty powers. They not only don't forget. They strike back."[21]

The invasion of Iraq has made us all far less safe. The longer U.S. troops stay, the more they will create opposition.

4. THE UNITED STATES IS NOT PREVENTING CIVIL WAR IN IRAQ.

Perhaps the greatest fear of many antiwar activists who now support the occupation is that the withdrawal of U.S. troops will lead to civil war. This idea has been encouraged repeatedly by supporters of the war. "Sectarian fault lines in Iraq are inexorably pushing the country towards civil war unless we actually intervene decisively to stem it," explained one U.S. Army official, making the case for a continued U.S. presence.[22] As veteran Middle East correspondent Robert Fisk points out, though, colonial powers have long used the rationale that they cannot withdraw, lest the natives collapse into civil war. "In 1920, [British prime minister David] Lloyd George warned of civil war in Iraq if the British Army left. Just as the Americans now threaten the Iraqis with civil war if they leave."[23]

But Washington is not preventing a civil war from breaking out. In fact, occupation authorities are deliberately pitting Kurds against Arabs, Shia against Sunni, and faction against faction to influence the character of the future government, following a classic divide-and-rule strategy.

Taking this idea to its logical extreme, *New York Times* columnist

Thomas L. Friedman argues, "We should arm the Shiites and Kurds and leave the Sunnis of Iraq to reap the wind." [24] Such arguments are not just the fantasy of keyboard warriors like Friedman, however. As the journalist A.K. Gupta notes, "the Pentagon is arming, training, and funding" militias in Iraq "for use in counter-insurgency operations." [25] Secretary of Defense Donald Rumsfeld said such commandos were among "the forces that are going to have the greatest leverage on suppressing and eliminating the insurgencies." [26]

In addition, the Iraqi constitution, drafted under intense pressure from occupation authorities, essentially enshrines sectarian divisions in Iraqi politics. As Phyllis Bennis argues, the constitutional referendum was "not a sign of Iraqi sovereignty and democracy taking hold, but rather a consolidation of U.S. influence and control," which "could transform the current violent political conflict into full-blown civil war between ethnic and religious communities."

> Instead of balancing the interests of Iraq's diverse population by referencing its long-dominant secular approaches, the draft constitution reflects, privileges and makes permanent the current occupation-fueled turn towards Islamic identity. . . . In historically secular Iraq, the shift in primary identity from "Iraqi" to "Sunni" or "Shia" (although Iraqi Kurdish identity was always stronger) happened largely in response to the U.S. invasion and occupation; it does not reflect historical cultural realities. The draft constitution promotes not just federalism as a national governing structure, but an extreme version of federalism in which all power not specifically assigned to the central government devolves automatically to the regional authorities—setting the stage for a potential division of Iraq largely along ethnic and religious lines. [27]

Not coincidentally, the Sunnis have the most to lose under this arrangement. Iraq's oil is concentrated in the Kurdish regions of northern Iraq and the Shia regions of the south, rather than in central Iraq, the location of Baghdad and the greatest concentration of Sunnis. This creates the basis for internal conflict over the distribution of earnings from Iraqi oil. Bennis points out that

> the federal government will administer the oil and gas from "current fields" with the revenues to be "distributed fairly in a [manner] compatible with the demographic distribution all over the country." But that guarantee refers only to oil fields already in use, leaving future exploitation of almost two-thirds of Iraq's known reserves (seventeen of eighty known fields, forty billion of its one hundred and fifteen billion barrels of known reserves), for foreign companies. . . . That means that future exploration and exploitation of Iraq's oil wealth will remain under the control of the regional authorities where the oil lies—the Kurdish-controlled North and the Shia-dominated South, insuring a future of impoverishment for the Sunni, secular and inter-mixed populations of Baghdad and Iraq's center, and sets the stage for a future of ethnic and religious strife.[28]

In addition, despite all of its rhetoric about confronting Islamic fundamentalism in Iraq, the United States has in fact encouraged it, bringing formerly marginalized fundamentalist parties such as the Dawa Party and the Iranian-backed Supreme Council for Islamic Revolution in Iraq into the Iraqi government.

5. THE UNITED STATES IS NOT CONFRONTING TERRORISM BY STAYING IN IRAQ.

Iraq has never been the center of a terrorist threat to the United States. Each month further evidence emerges that the Bush administration went to great lengths to suppress facts that undermined its case for war, while touting bogus evidence in its support. As the *New*

York Times reported in November 2005, "A top member of Al Qaeda in American custody was identified as a likely fabricator months before the Bush administration began to use his statements as the foundation for its claims that Iraq trained Al Qaeda members to use biological and chemical weapons, according to newly declassified portions of a Defense Intelligence Agency document."[29] The detainee, Ibn al-Shaykh al-Libi, was not alone in providing dubious "intelligence" that was then trumpeted by the Bush administration. In February 2002, DIA reported that al-Libi was most likely "intentionally misleading" U.S. officials and noted that Saddam Hussein "is wary of Islamic revolutionary movements" and that Baghdad "is unlikely to provide assistance to a group it cannot control."[30]

Al-Qaeda made its first appearance in Iraq only *after* the invasion, a predictable outcome of the U.S. occupation. In reality, the United States engaged in state terrorism under the pretext of fighting a terrorist threat that did not exist in Iraq, and in the process greatly increased the likelihood of individual and organizational terrorist acts targeting the United States or its proxies abroad.

Even more circular is the idea that the United States has to stay in Iraq until it "defeats" the resistance to the occupation. The occupation itself is the source of the resistance, a fact that even some of the people responsible for the war have been forced to acknowledge. The *Los Angeles Times* reported in October 2005 that some

> U.S. generals running the war in Iraq [had] presented a new assessment of the military situation in public comments and sworn testimony . . . : The one hundred and forty-nine thousand U.S. troops currently in Iraq are increasingly part of the problem. . . .
>
> The generals said the presence of U.S. forces was fueling the insurgency, fostering an undesirable dependency on American troops

among the nascent Iraqi armed forces and energizing terrorists across the Middle East.[31]

6. THE UNITED STATES IS NOT HONORING THOSE WHO DIED BY CONTINUING THE CONFLICT.

One of the most cynical reasons for staying in Iraq was advanced by President Bush in response to the growing public criticism over the mounting deaths of U.S. soldiers and the deliberate campaign by the administration to suppress images of the returning coffins. Speaking to a carefully targeted audience in Salt Lake City, Utah, where he fled to escape the protest of Cindy Sheehan, who lost her son, Casey, in Iraq on April 4, 2004, Bush made a rare public acknowledgment of the number of soldiers killed in Iraq and Afghanistan. "We owe them something," he said. "We will finish the task that they gave their lives for. We will honor their sacrifice by staying on the offensive against the terrorists."[32]

Sheehan herself had the best response to this attempt to manipulate people into supporting continued occupation, asking, "Why should I want one more mother to go through what I've gone through, because my son is dead? . . . I don't want him using my son's death or my family's sacrifice to continue the killing."[33]

The soldiers in Iraq have not died for a "noble cause," as Bush claims.[34] Whatever personal motivations may have brought them into the military, they died for oil, for empire, for power and profit. As Sheehan says of Casey, *"My son is a war victim, not a hero.* What is noble about what he's done? Going in and invading a country that's not a threat to the United States—that is not noble."[35]

More deaths and injuries of Iraqis and of U.S. soldiers will only compound the tragedy of the numerous lives already lost.

7. THE UNITED STATES IS NOT REBUILDING IRAQ.

The contractors now in Iraq are not there to help the people of Iraq but to help themselves, drawing on their close ties to influential politicians to secure contracts and profit from what Pratap Chatterjee rightly calls the "reconstruction racket." [36]

The reality is, Halliburton, Bechtel, and the other companies in Iraq are looting the country far more than they are rebuilding it. Iraqis have been forced to pay elevated prices to *import* oil, benefiting corporations like Halliburton subsidiary Kellogg, Brown & Root, while ordinary Iraqis have to stand in lines sometimes for days to buy gasoline. [37] Project after project remains unfinished. Hospitals are in shambles. Electricity is still at woefully inadequate levels.

As the journalist Naomi Klein eloquently observes, "The United States, having broken Iraq, is not in the process of fixing it. It is merely continuing to break the country and its people by other means, using not only F-16s and Bradleys, but now the less flashy weaponry" of economic strangulation. [38]

The Iraqi people are perfectly capable of rebuilding their own society, in fact far more so than foreign soldiers or contractors. To the extent that there have been any social services or security in the last two years, it is primarily Iraqis who have provided it. During the years of sanctions, Iraqis also showed their immense resourcefulness in holding together their badly damaged infrastructure. Iraqi engineers, teachers, and doctors have long been among the most educated and best trained in the Arab world. It is ultimately a racist worldview that believes Iraqis cannot rebuild or run their own country.

8. THE UNITED STATES IS NOT FULFILLING ITS OBLIGATION TO THE IRAQI PEOPLE FOR THE HARM AND SUFFERING IT HAS CAUSED.

Understandably, many opponents of the war now believe that the United States has an obligation to the Iraqi people and therefore has to stay to "clean up the mess it has created." MoveOn.org, which grabbed headlines and signed up millions of online members with its anti-Bush campaigning, refuses to call for withdrawal of troops from Iraq because, in the words of its executive director, Eli Pariser, "There are no good options in Iraq."[39] Using this same logic, leading antisanctions and antiwar groups such as the Education for Peace in Iraq Center have formally adopted positions in support of occupation, if somehow a more enlightened occupation, and therefore against immediate withdrawal.[40]

"Iraqis are paying a horrendous price for the good intentions of well-meaning conservatives who wanted to liberate them," writes *New York Times* columnist Nicholas Kristof. "Our mistaken invasion has left millions of Iraqis desperately vulnerable, and it would be inhumane to abandon them now. If we stay in Iraq, there is still some hope that Iraqis will come to enjoy security and better lives, but if we pull out we will be condemning Iraqis to anarchy, terrorism and starvation, costing the lives of hundreds of thousands of children over the next decade."[41]

Kristof can't imagine for a moment that the neoconservatives were not motivated by good intentions or ideals of liberation, but by baser motives of power projection and profit. But even if we set aside the question of motives, always subject to dispute, we must confront the bizarre logic of saying that the people who have devastated Iraq, who encouraged and enforced sanctions that cost the lives of hundreds of thousands of Iraqis in the *last* decade, who have failed at even the most basic responsibilities as an occupying power, who are the source of the instability in Iraq today, are the only ones who can protect Iraqis from hunger and anarchy. In no other area of our lives do we accept such logic, but when it comes to the crimes of empire, we are supposed to continually ignore history. The "doctrine of good intentions" exculpates all crimes.[42]

The reality, however, is that the U.S. occupation, rather than being a source of stability in Iraq, is the major source of instability and ongoing suffering.

Kristof is knocking down straw men when he argues that a "surgeon who botches an operation should not walk off and leave the patient on the table with a note: 'Oops. This didn't go as planned. Good luck, but I'm outta here.' "[43] As Howard Zinn has noted, the United States today can be more aptly characterized as a butcher than a surgeon.[44] But even if we accept Kristof's terms, we do not look to a surgeon with a long history of medical malpractice who grievously harmed a patient to undo the harm he or she caused, especially if the doctor's efforts to repair the initial damage have only made things worse. A doctor's first obligation is to keep patients "from harm and injustice," an oath the U.S. violates daily by its continued presence in Iraq.

Moreover, those calling for immediate withdrawal do not advocate a position of isolationism and of simply walking away from any obligation to the Iraqi people. Does the U.S. government have an obligation to the Iraqi people? Absolutely. An obligation for the crimes Washington supported for years when Saddam Hussein was an ally. For arming and supporting both sides in the brutal Iran-Iraq War. For the destruction of the 1991 Gulf War. For the use of depleted uranium munitions, cluster bombs, daisy cutters, and white phosphorus.[45] For the devastating sanctions. For the humiliation and deaths caused by the 2003 invasion, and for the great damage the occupation has caused since.

But the first step in meeting this obligation is to withdraw immediately.

If there were any genuine justice for the people of Iraq, not only would the politicians responsible for this unjust war face prosecution for their crimes, but the U.S. government would be required to pay reparations to the Iraqi people and to the families of U.S. soldiers who have been maimed and killed by its criminal actions. International justice groups will also need to find other ways of showing solidarity with the people of Iraq, much as they did during the years of sanctions, often in violation of laws preventing humanitarian assistance. This will entail, whenever possible, extending financial and political support to Iraqi trade unions, women's groups, and independent media—as some internationalist groups have already done in the post-invasion period, often at great personal risk. It will also entail supporting projects to eliminate the deadly legacy of land mines and depleted uranium munitions left behind by the United States and the United Kingdom. And it will mean supporting Iraqi efforts to fend off interference from outside powers, most notably the United States but also Turkey, Saudi Arabia, Kuwait, and Iran, all of which would be threatened by independent political struggles in Iraq; from the multinational oil companies, which will seek to undermine any efforts to limit their access to Iraqi oil; and from international financial institutions such as the World Bank and International Monetary Fund, which will try to punish Iraq if it takes an independent economic course.

In demanding an end to the U.S. occupation, we do not need to call for some other occupying power to replace the United States.

The United Nations, the most likely candidate in such a scenario, has shown through the years of the sanctions it imposed, the buildup to the war, and its endorsement of the U.S. occupation that it is not able or willing to confront U.S. power. On November 9, 2005, the UN Security Council voted yet again to extend the mandate of the occupation until December 31, 2006, in a unanimous vote on a resolution cosponsored by the United States, the United Kingdom, Japan, Denmark, and Romania. Among those voting for the resolution were Brazil, France, and Russia.[46]

Indeed, the United Nations has repeatedly allowed the United States to use the organization as a way of dressing the projection of U.S. power in multilateral clothing. The UN either serves U.S. purposes or it is declared "irrelevant," a situation that no nation or group of nations today is able to reverse. The Bush administration has a new message to the world. Washington is no longer simply saying, "You're either with us or against us," notes *New York Times* correspondent Serge Schmemann, but "something far more shrewd." The new position is: "Either you're with us, or you're irrelevant."[47]

Any outside power will not be accountable to the people of Iraq. And the United States is hardly alone in bearing responsibility for the suffering of the Iraqis. The United Nations is deeply implicated. The Arab League countries did nothing to protect the people of Iraq. Indeed, a number of its member states provided support for the invasions of Iraq in 1991 and 2003 while seeking to profit from the war and from the sanctions. Many countries besides the United States also supported Saddam Hussein, armed him, and protected him.

We should allow the people of Iraq to determine their own future. This means, as Naomi Klein has argued, that in addition to calling for an end to military occupation, we should be calling for an end to the *economic* occupation of Iraq and the cancellation of all debts that Iraq still owes from the previous regime (many of which still have not been forgiven).[48] If the Iraqis ask for outside assistance, that is their prerogative. But it is their decision, not ours, to make, and that decision can only be freely made if the United States, United Kingdom, and other occupying armies withdraw completely and end their economic, political, and military coercion of Iraq.

7.

OUT NOW

ON THE DAY that the number of U.S. soldiers killed in Iraq reached two thousand, President Bush boasted to an audience at Bolling Air Force Base, "We will never back down, never give in, and never accept anything less than complete victory." [1]

John F. Kennedy, Lyndon Johnson, and Richard Nixon made similar claims about the U.S. war against Vietnam. In the end, the U.S. ruling class discovered that its boasts about assured victory against "Communist insurgency" in Vietnam were empty.

The United States and its allies will be forced from Iraq in defeat or will at some point find a way, through overwhelming brutality, to impose the appearance of a "victory," perhaps under a new president who can remove the stain of illegitimacy that has marked the Bush administration's management of the war.

The real question, then, is: how many more will have to senselessly die before the conclusion of this bloody occupation?

"The Bush administration has said it cannot begin to withdraw a large number of troops until Iraqi security forces can operate independently in much of the country," the *New York Times* reports, noting that "some military experts say two years is not even enough" to draw down the more than one hundred and seventy thousand U.S.

and allied troops there.[2] Indeed, writes Eric Schmitt, "the military is coming to the realization that the war in Iraq could follow the path of other modern insurgencies and last a decade or so."[3]

On September 29, 2005, General John Abizaid, head of the U.S. Central Command, testified before the Senate Armed Services Committee that only one battalion of Iraqi soldiers was capable of carrying out effective operations independent of U.S. control, down from three battalions earlier in 2005.[4] Battalions in the Iraqi army have between three hundred and one thousand troops.[5] So the most generous interpretation is that, despite all the hype about the "great progress being made on the ground" in Iraq, no more than one thousand Iraqi soldiers are fully trained.[6]

"I think we are actually happy with the pace of the training," Stephen J. Hadley, Bush's national security advisor, told the *New York Times,* keeping to the administration's script. But as the *Times* acknowledged, even "other [Bush] administration officials have noted that the White House's claims a year ago of the number of troops and police who had been trained had proved to be overstated."[7]

Of course, such calculations are self-serving in one respect. The insurgency created by the occupation is being used to explain why the United States must continue the occupation, and assessments of Iraqi capabilities reflect the racist, colonial assumptions about the inability of Iraqis to manage their own affairs that are widespread in the military establishment. At the same time, the difficulty of training Iraqi soldiers is indicative of the profound problems facing the United States as it seeks to organize a security force that the local population regards as collaborationist.

Given the widespread opposition to the occupation, the high risks for Iraqis who collaborate with U.S. and other foreign troops, and the evidence of infiltration of the Iraqi police by Iraqis who also want to see U.S. troops leave, the U.S. strategy of Iraqization is likely, as with Vietnamization before it, to fail. The failures of Iraqization, however, will only provide a rationale for continued occupation unless the antiwar movement can compel the United States to withdraw.

An October 2005 study by the London-based International Institute for Strategic Studies suggested that the United States "will retain a sizeable force in Iraq even after President George W. Bush has left office," much as the war in Vietnam was passed from administration to administration. The next "administration will have forces in Iraq and a fairly large number for some years to come," Patrick Cronin, the director of the institute, told the *Financial Times*.[8]

From the beginning of the invasion of Iraq, the United States has been making plans to establish long-term military bases there. While Donald Rumsfeld has argued, "We have no intention at the present time of putting permanent bases in Iraq," top Bush officials told the *New York Times* just after the invasion that they were "planning a long-term military relationship with the emerging government of Iraq, one that would grant the Pentagon access to military bases and project American influence into the heart of the unsettled region."[9]

> American military officials, in interviews this week, spoke of maintaining perhaps four bases in Iraq that could be used in the future: one at the international airport just outside Baghdad; another at Tallil, near Nasiriya in the south; the third at an isolated airstrip called H-1 in the western desert, along the old oil pipeline that runs to Jordan; and the last at the Bashur air field in the Kurdish north. . . .
>
> "There will be some kind of a long-term defense relationship with a new Iraq, similar to Afghanistan," said one senior administration official. "The scope of that has yet to be defined—whether it will be full-up operational bases, smaller forward operating bases or just plain access."[10]

While Washington's public statements shifted as it became apparent how Iraqis felt about such permanent basing plans, all indications are that the U.S. government is still working toward a long-term military presence in Iraq and agreements that will grant access to Iraqi airspace and territory.

As the *Los Angeles Times* reports,

> John E. Pike, a defense analyst at GlobalSecurity.org, points to another indication. Although the United States is systematically training Iraqis to fight the insurgents, he notes, the Pentagon has not taken key steps—like making plans for acquiring tanks or aircraft—to build an Iraqi military capable of defending the country against its neighbors.
>
> To Pike that means that although the United States might reduce its troop level in Iraq, the fledgling nation, like Germany or South Korea, will require the sustained presence of a large American contingent, perhaps fifty thousand soldiers. "We are building the base structure to facilitate exactly [that]," he says.
>
> Whatever Iraqi politicians say publicly, Pike believes, in private many will prefer such a long-term U.S. presence, which might also provide insurance against a potential military coup.[11]

Much as Britain threatened Iraq in the first half of the twentieth century with the economic and political consequences of independence without its protection, the United States today is sending a clear message to Iraqi elites that they will need the support of the United States to survive. The *Christian Science Monitor* reports that "U.S. officials expect a new government—which is likely to be under fire from Day One—will not demand a fast pullout. 'I think the new government is going to look at all the problems, look into the abyss, and this is not going to be a problem,' says a senior U.S. diplomat."[12]

Iraq's importance as a strategic base for the projection of U.S. power in the Middle East is a serious concern for Washington. While the U.S. military maintains a security arrangement with Saudi Arabia that allows it access to Saudi territory and has kept some troops in the country for a "longstanding training program," it recently closed its military bases there in recognition of the widespread opposition they were causing, an unwelcome precedent.[13]

By invading Iraq, the Bush administration hoped to make Iraq a model "pro-Western" U.S. client regime, with bases that could be used to intimidate and "contain" neighboring states, especially Syria and Iran. To be driven from Iraq would not just mean a retreat but a serious reversal of U.S. plans in the region.

To force such a retreat, the antiwar movement in the United States and internationally will have to escalate its opposition significantly. In building such a movement, it will help to learn some of the lessons from the last major defeat of the United States in an imperial adventure, the war in Vietnam. The U.S. war on Vietnam ended because of a combination of five factors:

  (i) The mass resistance of the Vietnamese people to U.S. intervention.

 (ii) The resistance of U.S. soldiers and veterans, who sparked a rebellion against the war, provoking one military analyst to write, "The morale, discipline and battle-worthiness of the U.S. armed forces are, with a few salient exceptions, lower and worse than at any time in this century and possibly in the history of the United States."[14]

(iii) Domestic opposition on a scale that forced elites in the United States to recognize that they had lost the war at home, as well as in Vietnam.

(iv) International protest and opposition that isolated the United States politically and raised the costs of the war even further.

(v) The growing economic consequences of the war, which led to inflation and deficits that undermined the position of the U.S. economy.

Today, each of these factors is again in play, though none in its own right is sufficient and together they have not yet reached a critical mass strong enough to compel Washington to abandon the occupation.

The Iraqi resistance today is far more widespread than anyone in the U.S. military ever anticipated. U.S. planners thought that they were embarking on a quick, easy war. In an interview with Amy Goodman of *Democracy Now!*, retired brigadier general Janis Karpinski described the feeling right after the toppling of the Iraqi government. U.S. troops "all believed that they were going to come home after victory was declared" by President Bush on May 1, 2003.

> They allowed me to deploy to Iraq to join my units, to take command of the units, although I was told that the majority of the units, the soldiers, would be coming back home because the mission was complete.
>
> When I arrived in Kuwait, I was told that the units were going to be staying for an additional two months, because we were assigned a new mission for prison restoration and training, assisting the prison's experts up at Ambassador Bremer's headquarters in Baghdad with training Iraqi guards to conduct prison and detention operations. . . . Very quickly the two-month extension became a four-month extension, and then it became three hundred and sixty-five days, boots on the ground, for all of the units that were deployed.
>
> So, soldiers were sent to war with the full expectations that they would be home in six months or less, as they were repeatedly told at the mobilization stations in the United States, and once they were there, they couldn't get out.[15]

When General Eric K. Shinseki, then army chief of staff, testified in a Senate hearing before the war that "something on the order of several hundred thousand soldiers . . . would be required" for the occupation of Iraq, he was publicly contradicted by Deputy Defense Secretary Paul Wolfowitz and Defense Secretary Donald H. Rumsfeld.[16] Wolfowitz (who, following in the footsteps of Robert McNamara, soon abandoned his adventure in Iraq to become the president of the World Bank) called Shinseki's estimate "wildly off the mark," adding that the costs of occupation would also be low, since Iraqi oil revenue would pay for the occupation and "even countries like France will have a strong interest in assisting Iraq in reconstruction."[17]

"The emergence of the Iraqi insurgency stunned senior American commanders, who had planned for a short, sharp war against a uniformed army, with a bout of peacekeeping afterward," Dexter Filkins wrote in the *New York Times Magazine*.

> In response, American officers ordered their soldiers to bring Iraq back under control. They urged their men to go after the enemy, and they authorized a range of aggressive tactics. On a visit from his headquarters in Tikrit, Maj. Gen. Raymond Odierno, the commander of the Fourth Infantry Division, ordered . . . officers simply to "increase lethality."[18]

Such tactics have only fueled opposition to the occupation. Indeed, the pace of attacks on U.S. and allied troops has accelerated as the occupation has continued. "U.S. officials repeatedly have claimed progress during thirty-one months of war in Iraq, but the death toll of American troops has continued to rise inexorably, eroding support for the war and for the president who is so closely associated with it," the *Los Angeles Times* reported after the death of the two thousandth U.S. soldier in Iraq.

The death rate for American troops accelerated about eighteen months ago, around the war's first anniversary. The steadiness of the death rate since then, despite proclaimed political milestones and several strategies that U.S. military officials have employed to combat the insurgency, is among the most striking findings of a *Los Angeles Times* analysis of the fatalities.

The analysis compared the first one thousand deaths—from the beginning of the war in March 2003 through early September of last year—with the fatalities since. It showed a sharp increase in the number of deaths attributed to roadside bombs, which have overtaken rockets, mortars and gunfire as the greatest threat to U.S. troops and were responsible for more than half of the combat deaths in the past year.

It also documented the growing toll that the war has taken on National Guard and reserve units. Their soldiers now account for nearly one-third of the deaths, up from one-fifth.[19]

Those engaged in armed attacks on occupation forces are able to count on support from a significant section of the Iraqi population, much as in Vietnam. A secret poll conducted in August 2005 by the British Ministry of Defense that was leaked to the *Telegraph* newspaper in London found that between 45 and 65 percent of Iraqis support armed attacks on British and U.S. occupation forces.[20] "The line between civilians and insurgents is blurry," notes *New York Times* reporter Sabrina Tavernise. "When the streets empty out, the Americans know an attack is imminent. 'The population clearly gets the word—there's a network out there,' [Lt.] Colonel [Roger B.] Turner said at the Third Battalion's camp, in an old palace on the Euphrates."[21]

In addition to resistance from the Iraqi population, the U.S. government has also been forced to confront disaffection, as well as outright opposition, from the soldiers sent to fight the war, from military families, and from Iraq and Afghanistan war veterans. In 2005, the U.S. fell short of its military recruiting goals by a margin not seen since 1979.[22] "Today's conditions represent the most challenging conditions we have seen in recruiting in my thirty-three years in uniform," Major General Michael Rochelle, head of recruitment for the U.S. Army, said in 2005.[23] In particular, the army has seen a sharp drop-off in enlistment of African-American soldiers. In 2005, according to the *New York Times,*

> about 14 percent of new Army recruits were black, down from nearly 23 percent in 2001. Army officials say improved job opportunities in other fields is one reason. But a study commissioned by the Army last year also concluded that more young blacks were rejecting military service because they opposed the war, or feared dying in it.
>
> "More African-Americans identify having to fight for a cause they don't support as a barrier to military service," the study concluded.[24]

In schools and colleges across the United States, students and faculty in organizations such as the Campus Antiwar Network have confronted military recruiters, in some cases driving them off campus.[25] A Seattle parent-teacher-student association passed a resolution barring military recruiters from a local high school. "We want to show the military that they are not welcome by the P.T.S.A. in this building," explained Amy Hagopian, cochair of the organization at Seattle's Garfield High School. "We hope other P.T.S.A.'s will follow."[26] Parents and students have also campaigned against a provision in the USA PATRIOT Act that forces public schools to hand over student contact information to military recruiters unless parents specifically remove their child's name.

It is vital that we build a strong counter-recruitment movement to expose the lies used by the military to send working-class and poor children to war.[27] We must also lend our full support to the soldiers and reservists who are refusing to fight in Iraq.

In October 2003, Staff Sergeant Camilo Mejía, a member of the Florida National Guard, became the first soldier from the Iraq invasion to refuse to return to his post after a leave. "I cannot find a single good reason for having been there and having shot people and having been shot at," Mejía said. "People didn't want us there anymore, and we didn't want to be there."[28] Mejía served nine months in detention. Today, he is one of many veterans and soldiers speaking out against the war. Others are Navy Petty Officer Third Class Pablo Paredes, who also refused to redeploy to Iraq and was sentenced to three months of hard labor and demoted, and Sergeant Kevin Benderman, who was sentenced to fifteen months of detention for his conscientious objection to the war.[29]

Daryl Anderson, a soldier from Lawton, Kentucky, decided to cross into Canada and to seek protection, knowing well he might never be able to return to the United States, rather than go back to Iraq. "If I went back to Baghdad I would have been asked again to kill people, civilians, and I just couldn't do that anymore," he explained. "We're fighting people that we're supposed to help, but in fact they hate you and every time you walk down the street they shoot at you because you occupy their country. You're asked to get in their houses, in their businesses, block the roads, but you're an occupying power, you're messing up their daily life. You're not a liberator. You raid their houses and kill their family."[30]

"As the wars in Iraq and Afghanistan continue, counselors, anti-war activists and others who work with military families report a surge in calls from soldiers, sailors, airmen and Marines seeking help to withdraw from the service," the *St. Louis Post-Dispatch* reported early in 2005. "A growing number of soldiers and Marines in the all-volunteer force are seeking to be declared conscientious objectors," while between five and six thousand soldiers are "absent without leave." [31]

In Iraq, soldiers in the field have also refused orders from superiors. Twenty-three members of the 343rd Quartermaster Company, based in Rock Hill, South Carolina, were punished for refusing an October 2004 order to drive a fuel convoy from Tallil Air Base, in southern Iraq, to Taji, northwest of Baghdad.[32] "The soldiers complained that their vehicles had not been properly outfitted, their fuel was contaminated, and they were not being escorted by armed vehicles." They called the order a "suicide mission." [33]

During the Vietnam War, the U.S. government learned how quickly the discipline of an army fighting an unjust war can break down. Today, soldiers in the field can see the contradictions between the claims of their officers and especially the politicians who sent them to war and the reality of the conflict on the ground. They now know that Iraq had no weapons of mass destruction and posed no imminent threat. And as the Iraqi resistance to occupation grows, more soldiers have come to see that they are fighting not to liberate Iraqis but to "pacify" them. To end this war, more will need to follow their conscience, like Mejía and the other soldiers who have refused to die—or kill—for a lie.

On the international front, the Bush administration has grown ever more isolated. The list of countries that were once part of the so-called coalition of the willing has declined steadily as domestic opposition has pressured governments to withdraw troops. Bulgaria, the Dominican Republic, Honduras, Hungary, Moldova, New Zealand, Nicaragua, the Philippines, Portugal, South Korea, Spain, Thailand, and Tonga have all withdrawn their forces from Iraq.[34] In

March 2004, the socialist candidate José Luis Rodríguez Zapatero defeated Spain's incumbent prime minister, José María Aznar, who had close ties to President Bush. Zapatero immediately withdrew Spain's forces from Iraq and announced that the Spanish government would never again send troops to war "behind the backs of its citizens." [35]

"Anti-Americanism is deeper and broader now than at any time in modern history," notes the Pew Global Attitudes Project.[36] The term *anti-Americanism* is misleading, however. Beyond the fact that the Americas should not be equated, as they so often are, with the United States, opinion polls demonstrate consistently that people do not reject U.S. culture or hate the people of the country. Rather, they oppose U.S. government policies, particularly support for Israel, and its invasion and occupation of Afghanistan and Iraq.

The level of international opposition to the war has led some business leaders and elites to begin to talk openly about the harm the occupation of Iraq is causing, citing rapidly growing deficits, inflation risks, and the declining image of U.S.-based corporations and products abroad.[37] Prominent hawks, such as William Odom, a director of the National Security Agency during the Reagan administration, have also started to speak out against the war. According to Odom, "Staying . . . damages our credibility more than leaving" Iraq.[38] Several former officials of the current administration have also spoken out about the rush to war in Iraq and the emptiness of the president's rhetoric about progress in the occupation.

But even more significantly, popular opposition to the war is growing. Opinion polls show that a majority of the population now opposes the decision to attack Iraq. A majority also wants troops brought home, either immediately or in the near future, with negative opinions of Bush, the Republicans in Congress, and the war continuing to grow.[39] Asked in a September 2005 poll if they consider themselves members of the antiwar movement, 23 percent of respondents answered yes, a figure that translates into roughly fifty million people above the age of sixteen, based on the latest U.S. Census Bureau figures.[40]

More than one hundred thousand people marched in Washington, D.C., on September 24, 2005, in the largest demonstrations

TABLE 2

RATING OF PRESIDENT BUSH—HANDLING OF IRAQ
"Overall, how would you rate the job President Bush has done in handling the issue of Iraq over the last several months?"
Base: All Adults

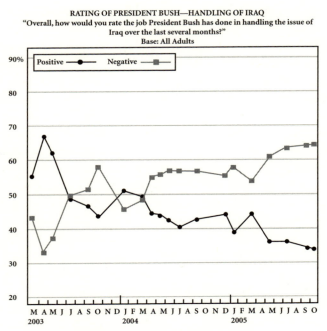

The Harris Poll ® #79, October 25, 2005
"Majority of U.S. Adults Feel Military Action in Iraq Was the Wrong Thing to Do, According to Latest Harris Poll."
Harris Interactive Inc. All rights reserved.[41]

since the invasion of Iraq. Participants drew connections between the war and the government's criminally negligent response to Hurricane Katrina, noting that three thousand Louisiana and three thousand eight hundred Mississippi National Guard troops, as well as equipment that could have been used for relief efforts, were in Iraq when the storm hit.[42] Protesters carried placards reading "Make Levees, Not War." Many came to the march after being encouraged to speak up by Cindy Sheehan's courageous stand against the war outside President Bush's vacation home in Crawford, Texas, the month before.

But none of the existing currents of opposition is strong enough yet to end the war. Each will have to build independently, while also forging critical alliances. Along the way, the U.S. left in particular needs far greater clarity about the reasons for the war, the political context of the war, and an effective strategy for ending it.

The U.S. left made a terrible and costly mistake in supporting the presidential campaign of John Kerry, giving up its independence and political principles to support a prowar candidate. Kerry called for sending more troops to Iraq, insisting that "it would be unthinkable now for us to retreat in disarray and leave behind a society deep in strife and dominated by radicals."[43] Kerry also asserted that he would still have voted to authorize President Bush to invade Iraq even if he knew Iraq did not have weapons of mass destruction, a position that he only clearly retracted after losing the election and when popular sentiment had turned strongly against the war.[44]

But rather than learn from the experience, many in the antiwar movement have continued to hold illusions about the Democrats, hoping they will somehow become the standard-bearer for the anti-occupation message. While some Democrats, for opportunistic reasons, will certainly come to see that they can gain votes by challenging Bush, they will do so not to lead the antiwar movement but to put themselves at the front of it and direct it back into electoral channels. The Democrats, who not only voted for the war but have repeatedly voted to fund it, have tactical, not principled, differences from the Republicans, believing that, in the words of the *Washington Post*, "success in Iraq at this point is too important for the country." [45]

In fact, rather than arguing for troops to come home, a number of leading Democrats, such as senators Joseph Lieberman and Hillary Clinton, are seeking to outflank Bush from the right by calling for more troops in Iraq. "We need more troops in Iraq now," Lieberman, Democrat of Connecticut, told the *Hartford Courant* editorial board.[46] Many liberals campaigned heavily for Clinton's run for Senate in New York. But, as the *New York Times* observes, "In recent speeches and interviews, as well as in votes in the Senate, she has emerged as a staunch ally of the armed services and a strong proponent of a forceful American military presence abroad. On Iraq, for example, she has stood by her vote authorizing the president to wage war and has argued for a greater troop presence there." [47]

When Representative John P. Murtha, a Democrat from Pennsylvania, broke ranks to call for pulling troops out of Iraq, the reaction of his party was telling. Leading party members immediately distanced themselves from Murtha's position. "Jack Murtha went out and spoke for Jack Murtha," not the party, Representative Rahm Emanuel stated. When asked to explain the Democrats' position on the war, he said, "At the right time, we will have a position." [48]

Journalist Jeremy Scahill is absolutely right when he argues that "the Democrats are not an opposition party, nor are they an antiwar party—never were. At best, they are a loyal opposition."

> None of the horrors playing out in Iraq today would be possible without the Democratic Party. And no matter how hard some party leaders try to deny it, this is their war too and will remain so until every troop is withdrawn. There is no question that the Bush admin-

istration is one of the most corrupt, violent and brutal in the history of this country but that doesn't erase the serious responsibility the Democrats bear for the bloodletting in Iraq. As disingenuous as the administration's claims that Iraq had WMDs is the flimsy claim by Democratic lawmakers that they were somehow duped into voting for the war. The fact is that Iraq posed no threat to the United States in 2003 any more than it did in 1998 when President Clinton bombed Baghdad. John Kerry and his colleagues knew that. The Democrats didn't need false intelligence to push them into over-throwing Saddam Hussein's regime. It was their policy; a policy made the law of the land not under George W. Bush, but under President Bill Clinton when he signed the 1998 Iraq Liberation Act, formally initiating the process of regime change in Iraq.[49]

In reality, the war in Iraq and the broader "war on terror" are based on a bipartisan consensus. The Democrats and Republicans agree on the fundamental right of the United States to intervene in other countries, to topple regimes it dislikes, and to be a global hege-monic power. The Democrats will use force "without asking anyone's permission" boasts Democratic leader Joseph R. Biden Jr., of Delaware, in the party's typical "me too" fashion.[50]

Some liberals have staked their opposition to the war in Iraq on the idea that Iraq is a "distraction." The problem with this line of ar-gument is that it accepts that Bush is now waging an otherwise legit-imate war. Bush's agenda has absolutely nothing to do with fighting terrorism or reducing its likelihood, however. The Bush administra-tion is pushing a series of foreign policy objectives that it had before September 11. These are not defensive but offensive goals, seeking to expand U.S. economic and military power abroad. The "war on ter-ror" rubric is a way of selling decades of war through racism and the demonization of Arabs and of Islam, much as anticommunism was used as an ideological rationale for U.S. aims in Africa, Central Asia, Latin America, and the Middle East.[51]

Any movement to end the war in Iraq will need to mount a direct challenge to both major parties and the whole ideological framework used to sell the war. The antiwar movement needs to assert its independence from the Democrats and challenge the broad consensus that underlies the war on terror, especially U.S. exceptionalism, Islamophobia, anti-Arab racism, and liberal imperialism.

In addition, we need more politics in the antiwar movement, not less. The common idea that people in "the heartland" or "Middle America" or in military families need to be protected from politics is elitist and misguided. It is not just radicals or progressives who understand that there are connections between the U.S. occupation of Iraq and longstanding U.S. support for Israel and for numerous Arab regimes that repress their populations but preserve "stability" in the region. Soldiers and military families themselves are raising questions about oil, imperialism, racism, and the real reasons behind the war. Indeed, soldiers have also expressed empathy for the Iraqis who are resisting them. "If someone invaded Texas, we'd do the same thing," observed Lt. Col. Kim Keslung.[52]

The stronger the consciously anti-imperialist current in the antiwar movement, the stronger the movement to end the war will be, and the greater chance we will have to bring about the fundamental change needed to stop future wars.

The great satirist and novelist Mark Twain summed up the politics of anti-imperialism very effectively at the time of his opposition to the U.S. occupation of the Philippines: "I am opposed to having the eagle putting its talons on any other land."[53] We need to revive and popularize this sentiment, and at the same time we need to address the economic roots of war in a system with completely irrational priorities, a system that sends people to die and kill to control a declining oil supply rather than develop a humane and environmentally sustainable system of production and transportation; that leaves people vulnerable to environmental disasters such as Hurricane Katrina and then abandons them to die, while spending hundreds of billions of dollars to occupy Iraq and to redraw the map of the Middle East; and that is forcing Iraq, one of the world's most oil-rich countries, to import oil from its neighbors, at the cost of some two hundred million dollars a month.[54]

We need to highlight the class aspects of this war. Who is fighting, who is dying, who is sending the soldiers to fight? Why are there billions of dollars available for this war, yet schools are crumbling and forty-five million people in the United States do not have any health insurance, while tens of millions more have inadequate or only partial coverage?

The wars in Afghanistan and Iraq have "obscured the fact that many people in this country are still in need," observes historian Howard Zinn. "We need to dig under the rubble of war and point out that the Bush administration is using the war as a cover for worsening the income gap in this country, while paying no attention to the problems of most of the American people, while enriching corporations. I think concentrating on the class issue, concentrating on the benefits being given to corporations, is critical."[55]

But Zinn raises an even more urgent point: "The left is in a position of continually opposing war after war after war, without getting at the root of the problem—which is the economic system under which we live, which needs war and makes war inevitable."[56]

The United States is spending one billion dollars a week in its occupation of Iraq, excluding the cost of "reconstruction" (the government's and the media's euphemism for massive federal subsidies to corporations close to the Bush administration). "If the Department of Defense were a business, they'd be out of business," commented David Walker, the Government Accountability Office comptroller general. "They have absolutely atrocious financial management. . . . I can't understand how we're spending $1 billion a week."[57] This is in addition to the tens of billions of dollars already allocated for the invasion of Iraq, the tens of billions the United States pays to maintain its massive military arsenal in the Middle East and Asia, and the tens of billions the government spends to support "allies" such as Israel, Egypt, Jordan, Turkey, Saudi Arabia, and the Emirates.

While the wars in Afghanistan and Iraq have now cost more than three hundred billion dollars and the Pentagon's annual budget is more than four hundred billion dollars, budgets for early childhood education programs, health care, day care, libraries, and basic social services are being slashed drastically around the country.[58] City after city and state after state are reporting fiscal crises.

The corporate looting of Iraq is simply an extension of the looting at home, which has seen more and more wealth going from workers to the very rich. This economic war on poor and working people is also going hand in hand with a major attack on civil liberties, particularly those of immigrants and Muslims, who face greater risk of false arrest, harassment, deportation, and detention.[59] The antiwar movement needs not only to defend these communities but to build a membership—and a public leadership—that is representative and inclusive of them.

We need to involve larger numbers of people facing budget cuts, attacks on their jobs and unions, and violations of their civil liberties, as well as more and more family and friends of those in the military, to demand all foreign troops in Iraq be brought home now.

A number of unions, many working with the organization U.S.

Labor Against the War, have passed resolutions that can be used as models for raising the issue of the war and occupation in our workplaces. Teamsters Local 705 in Chicago provides a constructive example of how we can link the war at home and the war abroad:

> Whereas, we value the lives of our sons and daughters, of our brothers and sisters more than Bush's control of Middle East oil profits;
>
> Whereas, we have no quarrel with the ordinary working-class men, women, and children of Iraq who will suffer the most in any war;
>
> Whereas, the billions of dollars being spent to stage and execute this invasion means billions taken away from our schools, hospitals, housing, and social security;
>
> Whereas, Bush's drive for war serves as a cover and a distraction for the sinking economy, corporate corruption, lay-offs, Taft-Hartley (used against the locked out ILWU [International Longshore Workers' Union] longshoremen);
>
> Whereas, Teamsters Local 705 is known far and wide as fighters for justice;
>
> Be It Resolved that Teamsters Local 705 stands firmly against Bush's drive for war;
>
> Further Resolved that the Teamsters Local 705 Executive Board publicize this statement; and seek out other unions, labor and community activists interested in promoting anti-war activity in the labor movement and community.[60]

Indeed, views of the war in Iraq, like that in Vietnam, are correlated strongly to race and class. The less money you earn, the more likely you are to oppose the war.[61] Seventy-nine percent of African-Americans think the war in Iraq was a mistake.[62] Approval of President Bush among African-Americans is 2 percent.[63]

Millions of people sympathize with the aims of the antiwar

movement but have not yet been mobilized for actions. We need to involve these wider audiences in our movement and to connect local actions with coordinated national actions that can help people to overcome the pervasive sense of isolation and atomization that so many feel.

To make our demonstrations effective, we will have to, as the civil rights activist John Lewis once urged, no longer "confine our marching to Washington." [64] National demonstrations are vital, but cannot substitute for local actions that target symbols and institutions of the war. We should also no longer confine our civil disobedience to the day after major mobilizations, when most protesters have gone home. This strategy only confirms the idea of the antiwar movement as being an enlightened minority, set apart from the mass of people who must be a part of ending the war.

As with the movement to end the war on Vietnam, we will have to fight on many fronts: supporting counter-recruitment, confronting government and military officials about the human costs of this war and the lies they use to justify it, exposing war profiteers, encouraging and protecting soldiers who speak out and who resist their orders or service, working with veterans groups such as Iraq Veterans Against the War and military families' groups like Gold Star Families for Peace, and all along arguing patiently yet urgently with everyone around us that we need to end the occupation now.

AFTERWORD
by Howard Zinn

ON AMERICAN EXCEPTIONALISM

THE NOTION OF AMERICAN exceptionalism is not new. It started as early as 1630 in the Massachusetts Bay Colony when Governor John Winthrop uttered the words that, centuries later, would be quoted by Ronald Reagan. Winthrop called the Massachusetts Bay Colony a "city on a hill." [1] Reagan embellished a little, calling it a "shining city on a hill." [2]

The idea of a city on a hill is heartwarming. It suggests what George W. Bush has spoken of: the United States is a beacon of liberty and democracy. People can look to us, and learn from and emulate us.

In reality, we have never been just a city on a hill. A few years after Governor Winthrop uttered his famous words, the people in the city on a hill moved out to massacre the Pequot Indians. Here's a description by William Bradford, an early settler, of Captain John Mason's attack on a Pequot village:

> Those that scaped the fire, were slaine with the sword; some hewed to peeces, others run through with their rapiers, so as they were quickly

dispatchte and very few escaped. It was conceived they thus destroyed about 400, at this time. It was a fearfull sight to see them thus frying in the fyre, and the streams of blood quenching the same, and horrible was the stinck and sente ther of; they gave the prays thereof to God, who had wrought so wonderfully for them, thus to inclose their enemies in their hands, and give them so speedy a victory over so proud and insulting an enimie.[3]

The kind of massacre described by Bradford occurred again and again as the colonists marched west to the Pacific and south to the Gulf of Mexico. (In fact our celebrated war of liberation—the American Revolution—was disastrous for the Indians. Colonists had been restrained from encroaching on the Indian territory by the British and the boundary set up in the Proclamation of 1763. U.S. independence wiped out that boundary.)

Expansion into another territory, occupying that territory, and dealing harshly with people who resist that occupation has been a persistent fact of U.S. history from the first settlers to the present day. And it was often accompanied from very early on by a particular form of American exceptionalism: U.S. expansion is divinely ordained. On the eve of the war with Mexico in the middle of the nineteenth century, just after the United States annexed Texas, the editor and writer John O'Sullivan coined the famous phrase "manifest destiny." He said it was "our manifest destiny to overspread the continent allotted by Providence for the free development of our yearly multiplying millions."[4]

Providence continued to be involved in U.S. expansion. At the beginning of the twentieth century, when the United States invaded the Philippines, President McKinley said that the decision to take the Philippines came one night when he got down on his knees and prayed and God told him to take the country.[5]

Invoking God has been a habit for presidents throughout U.S. history, but George Bush has made a specialty of it. For a recent article in the Israeli newspaper *Ha'aretz,* the reporter talked with Palestinian leaders who had met with Bush. One of them reported that Bush told him: "God told me to strike at Al Qaeda, and I struck them, and then he instructed me to strike at Saddam, which I did, and now I am determined to solve the problem in the Middle East." [6] It's hard to know if the quote is authentic, especially because it is so literate. But it certainly is consistent with Bush's oft-expressed claims.

Divine ordination is a very dangerous idea, especially when combined with military power. With God's approval, you need no human standard of morality. Anyone today who claims the support of God might be embarrassed to recall that the Nazi storm troopers had on their belts *"Gut mit uns"* (God with us).

When the government of the United States—a nation with ten thousand nuclear weapons, military bases in a hundred different countries, and warships on every sea—assures us it gets its power from God, the world is in danger.

Not every U.S. leader claimed divine sanction, but the idea persisted that the United States was uniquely justified in using its power to expand throughout the world. In 1945, at the end of World War II, Henry Luce, the owner of a vast chain of media enterprises—*Time, Life, Fortune*—declared that this would be "the American Century," that victory in the war gave the United States the right "to exert upon the world the full impact of our influence, for such purposes as we see fit and by such means as we see fit." [7]

This confident prophecy was acted out all through the rest of the twentieth century. Almost immediately after World War II, the United States penetrated the oil regions of the Middle East by special arrangements with Saudi Arabia. It established military bases in Japan, Korea, the Philippines, and a number of Pacific islands. In the next decades it orchestrated right-wing coups in Iran, Guatemala, and Chile, and gave military aid to various dictatorships in the Caribbean. It soon had military bases all over the world, and in an attempt to establish a foothold in Southeast Asia it invaded Vietnam and bombed Laos and Cambodia.

The existence of the Soviet Union, even with its acquisition of nuclear weapons, did not block this expansion. In fact, the exaggerated threat of "world communism" gave the United States a powerful justification for expanding all over the globe, and soon it had military bases in a hundred countries. Presumably, only the United States stood in the way of the Soviet conquest of the world.

Can we believe that it was the existence of the Soviet Union that brought about the aggressive militarism of the United States? If so, how do we explain all that violent expansion before 1917? A hundred years before the Bolshevik Revolution, U.S. armies were annihilating Indian tribes, clearing the great expanse of the West in an early example of what we now call "ethnic cleansing." And with the continent conquered, the nation began to look overseas.

On the eve of the twentieth century, as U.S. armies moved into Cuba and the Philippines, American exceptionalism was not always exclusive. The nation was willing, indeed eager, to join the small group of Western imperial powers, which one day it would supersede. Senator Henry Cabot Lodge wrote at the time: "The great nations are rapidly absorbing for their future expansion and their present defence all the waste places of the earth. . . . As one of the great nations of the world, the United States must not fall out of the line of march."[8]

American exceptionalism was never more clearly expressed than by Secretary of War Elihu Root, who in 1899 declared: "The American soldier is different from all other soldiers of all other countries since the world began. He is the advance guard of liberty and justice, of law and order, and of peace and happiness."[9] At the time he was saying this, U.S. soldiers in the Philippines were starting a bloodbath that would take the lives of six hundred thousand Filipinos.

The idea that America is different because its military actions are for the benefit of others becomes particularly persuasive when it is put forth by leaders presumed to be liberals, progressives. For instance, Woodrow Wilson, always high on the list of "liberal" presidents, labeled both by scholars and the popular culture as an "idealist," was ruthless in the use of military power against weaker nations. He sent the navy to bombard and occupy the Mexican port of Veracruz in 1914 because the Mexicans had arrested some U.S. sailors. He sent the marines into Haiti in 1915, and when the Haitians resisted, thousands were killed.

The following year, U.S. marines occupied the Dominican Republic. The occupations of Haiti and the Dominican Republic lasted many years. And Wilson, who had been reelected in 1916 saying that "there is such a thing as a nation being so right that it does not need to convince others by force that it is right," soon sent young U.S. soldiers into the slaughterhouse of the European war.[10]

Theodore Roosevelt was considered a progressive. Indeed, he ran for president on the Progressive Party ticket in 1912. But he was a lover of war, a supporter of the conquest of the Philippines, indeed had congratulated the general who wiped out a Filipino village of six hundred people in 1906. He had promulgated the 1904 "Roosevelt Corollary" to the Monroe Doctrine, which justified the occupation of small countries in the Caribbean as bringing them "stability."

During the Cold War, many U.S. "liberals" became caught up in a kind of hysteria about the Soviet threat, which was certainly real in Eastern Europe, but was greatly exaggerated as a threat to Western Europe or the United States. During the period of McCarthyism, the Senate's quintessential liberal, Hubert Humphrey, proposed detention camps for suspected subversives who, in times of "national emergency," could be held without trial.[11]

After the disintegration of the Soviet Union and the end of the Cold War, terrorism replaced communism as the justification for expansion. Terrorism was real, but its threat was magnified to the point of hysteria, permitting excessive military action abroad and curtailment of civil liberties at home.

The idea of American exceptionalism persisted as the first President Bush declared, following up on Henry Luce's prediction, that the nation was about to embark on a "new American Century."[12] Though the Soviet Union was gone, the policy of military intervention abroad did not end. Bush Senior invaded Panama and then went to war against Iraq.

The terrible attacks of September 11 gave a new impetus to the idea that the United States was uniquely responsible for the security of the world, defending us all against terrorism as it once did against communism. President George W. Bush carried the idea of American exceptionalism to its limits by putting forth, in his national security strategy, the principles of preemptive war, carried on unilaterally, with unchallenged U.S. military supremacy.

This was a repudiation of the United Nations Charter, which is based on the idea that security is a collective matter, and that war could only be justified in self-defense. We might note that the Bush doctrine also violates the principles laid out at Nuremberg, when Nazi leaders were convicted and hanged for aggressive war, preemptive war, far from self-defense.

Bush's national security strategy, its bold statement that the United States is uniquely responsible for peace and democracy in the world—this stark declaration of American exceptionalism—has been shocking to many. But it is not really a dramatic departure from the historical practice of the United States, which for a long time has acted as an aggressor, bombing and invading other countries (Vietnam, Cambodia, Laos, Grenada, Panama, Iraq), insisting on maintaining nuclear and non-nuclear supremacy. Preemption and unilateralism are familiar characteristics of U.S. foreign policy.

Sometimes bombings and invasions have been cloaked as international action by bringing in the United Nations, as in Korea, or the North Atlantic Treaty Organization, as in Serbia. But basically our wars have been U.S. enterprises. It was Bill Clinton's secretary of state, Madeleine Albright, who said at one point that the United States "will behave, with others, multilaterally when we can and unilaterally when we must." [13] Henry Kissinger, echoing this, said, with his customary solemnity, that "it is not in the American national interest to establish pre-emption as a universal principle available to every nation." [14] Exceptionalism was never clearer.

Some liberals in this country who are opposed to Bush nevertheless accept his principles in foreign affairs. It is clear that September 11 had a powerful psychological effect on everybody in America, and for certain liberal intellectuals, a kind of hysterical reaction to September 11 has distorted their ability to think clearly about our nation's role in the world.

In a recent issue of the liberal magazine the *American Prospect,* the editors write:

> The first imperative of America's defense and foreign policy, however, is to protect our security, and today Islamist terrorists with global reach pose the greatest immediate threat to our lives and lib-

erty. . . . When facing a substantial, immediate, and provable threat, the United States has both the right and the obligation to strike preemptively and, if need be, unilaterally against terrorists or states that support them.[15]

"Preemptively, and if need be, unilaterally." That is the Bush doctrine. The writers qualify what would otherwise be obviously embarrassing by putting in the words "facing a substantial, immediate, and provable threat." But those who decide whether a threat is in fact substantial, immediate, and provable will not be the liberal intellectuals who formulated this but the people who run the government of the United States.

It seems that the idea of American exceptionalism—that the United States alone has the right, whether by divine sanction or moral obligation, to bring civilization, or democracy, or liberty to the rest of the world by violence if necessary—finds acceptance on all sides of the political spectrum.

The idea is not challenged because the history of U.S. expansion in the world is not a history that is taught very much in our educational system. Our universities have specialties in something called "diplomatic history," in which the history of our foreign policy is indeed treated diplomatically.

A couple of years ago, Bush addressed the Philippines Congress and said, "America is proud of its part in the great story of the Filipino people. Together our soldiers liberated the Philippines from colonial rule."[16] The president apparently never learned the story of the bloody conquest of the Philippines.

And last year, when the Mexican ambassador to the United Nations said something undiplomatic about how the United States has been treating Mexico as its "backyard," he was immediately reprimanded by Colin Powell. Powell, denying the accusation, said, "We have too much of a history that we have gone through together."[17] (Had he not learned about the Mexican War or the military forays into Mexico?) The ambassador was soon removed from his post.[18]

The major newspapers, television news shows, and radio talk shows appear not to know history, or prefer to forget our history. There was an outpouring of praise for Bush's second inaugural address all through the press, including the so-called liberal press (the *Washington Post*, the *New York Times*). The editorial writers eagerly embraced the words uttered by George Bush about "spreading liberty" in the world, as if they were ignorant of the history of such claims, as if the news from Iraq over the past two years that suggests otherwise were meaningless.[19]

Only a couple of days before Bush uttered those words about spreading liberty in the world, the *New York Times* published a photo of a crouching, bleeding Iraqi girl. She was screaming. Her parents, taking her somewhere in their car, had just been shot to death by nervous U.S. soldiers.[20]

One of the consequences of American exceptionalism is that the U.S. government considers itself exempt from legal and moral standards accepted by other nations in the world. There is a long list of such instances: the refusal to sign the Kyoto Protocol regulating the pollution of the environment, the refusal to strengthen the convention on biological weapons. The United States has failed to join the hundred or more nations that have agreed to ban land mines, in spite of the appalling statistics on amputations performed on children mutilated by those mines. It refuses to ban the use of napalm and cluster bombs. It insists that it must not be subject, as are other countries, to the jurisdiction of the International Criminal Court.

What is the answer to the insistence on American exceptionalism? Those of us in the United States and in the world who don't accept it must declare very forcibly that the ethical norms concerning peace and human rights should be observed. The children of the world should all be seen as part of one family. It should be understood that the children of Iraq, of China, of Africa, children everywhere in the world, have the same right to life as children in the United States.

These are fundamental moral principles. If our government doesn't uphold them, the citizenry must. At certain times in recent history, imperial powers—the British in India and East Africa, the Belgians in the Congo, the French in Algeria, the Dutch and French in Southeast Asia, the Portuguese in Angola—have reluctantly surrendered their possessions and swallowed their pride when they were forced to by massive resistance.

Fortunately, there are people all over the world who believe that human beings everywhere deserve the same rights to life and liberty. On February 15, 2003, on the eve of the invasion of Iraq, ten to fifteen million people in more than sixty countries around the world demonstrated against that war.

There is a growing refusal to accept U.S. domination and the idea of American exceptionalism. Recently, when the State Department issued its annual report listing countries guilty of torture and other human rights abuses, there were indignant responses from around the world commenting on the absence of the United States from that list. A Turkish newspaper said, "There is not even a mention of the incidents in Abu Ghraib prison in Iraq. . . . Of course, there is no mention of Guantánamo, either."[21] A newspaper in Sydney, Australia, pointed out that the United States sends suspects—people who have not been tried or found guilty of anything—to prisons in Morocco, Egypt, Libya, and Uzbekistan, countries that the State Department itself says use torture.[22]

Here in the United States, despite the media's failure to report it, there is a growing resistance to the war in Iraq. Public opinion polls show that at least half the citizenry no longer believes in the war. Perhaps most significant is that among the armed forces and families of those in the armed forces, there is more and more opposition to the war.

After the horrors of the First World War, Albert Einstein said, "Nothing will end war unless the people themselves refuse to war." [23] We are now seeing the refusal of soldiers to fight, the refusal of families to let their loved ones go to war, the insistence of the parents of high school kids that recruiters stay away from their schools. These incidents, occurring more and more frequently, may finally, as happened in the case of Vietnam, make it impossible for the government to continue the war, and it will come to an end.

The true heroes of our history are those individuals who refused to accept that we have a special claim to morality and the right to exert our force on the rest of the world. I think of William Lloyd Garrison, the abolitionist. On the masthead of his antislavery newspaper, the *Liberator*, were these words: "Our country is the world— Our countrymen are mankind." [24]

APPENDIX: ISTANBUL DECLARATION

DECLARATION OF THE JURY OF CONSCIENCE
WORLD TRIBUNAL ON IRAQ
ISTANBUL, TURKEY
JUNE 27, 2005

IN FEBRUARY 2003, weeks before an illegal war was initiated against Iraq, millions of people protested in the streets of the world. That call went unheeded. No international institution had the courage or conscience to stand up to the threat of aggression of the U.S. and UK governments. No one could stop them. It is two years later now. Iraq has been invaded, occupied, and devastated. The attack on Iraq is an attack on justice, on liberty, on our safety, on our future, on us all. We, people of conscience, decided to stand up. We formed the World Tribunal on Iraq (WTI) to demand justice and a peaceful future.

The legitimacy of the World Tribunal on Iraq is located in the collective conscience of humanity. This, the Istanbul session of the WTI, is the culmination of a series of twenty hearings held in different cities of the world focusing on the illegal invasion and occupation of Iraq. The conclusions of these sessions and/or inquiries held in Barcelona, Brussels, Copenhagen, Genoa, Hiroshima, Istanbul, Lisbon, London, Mumbai, New York, Östersund, Paris, Rome, Seoul, Stockholm, Tunis, various cities in Japan and Germany are appended to this Declaration in a separate volume.

We, the Jury of Conscience, from ten different countries, met in Istanbul. We heard fifty-four testimonies from a Panel of Advocates and Witnesses who came from across the world, including from Iraq, the United States, and the United Kingdom.

The World Tribunal on Iraq met in Istanbul from 24–26 June 2005. The principal objective of the WTI is to tell and disseminate the truth about the Iraq War, underscoring the accountability of those responsible and underlining the significance of justice for the Iraqi people.

I. OVERVIEW OF FINDINGS

1. The invasion and occupation of Iraq was and is illegal. The reasons given by the U.S. and UK governments for the invasion and occupation of Iraq in March 2003 have proven to be false. Much evidence supports the conclusion that a major motive for the war was to control and dominate the Middle East and its vast reserves of oil as a part of the U.S. drive for global hegemony.

2. Blatant falsehoods about the presence of weapons of mass destruction in Iraq and a link between Al Qaeda terrorism and the Saddam Hussein régime were manufactured in order to create public support for a "preemptive" assault upon a sovereign independent nation.

3. Iraq has been under siege for years. The imposition of severe inhumane economic sanctions on 6 August 1990, the establishment of no-fly zones in the Northern and Southern parts of Iraq, and the concomitant bombing of the country were all aimed at degrading and weakening Iraq's human and material resources and capacities in order to facilitate its subsequent invasion and occupation. In this enterprise the U.S. and British leaderships had the benefit of a complicit UN Security Council.

4. In pursuit of their agenda of empire, the Bush and Blair governments blatantly ignored the massive opposition to the war expressed by millions of people around the world. They embarked upon one of the most unjust, immoral, and cowardly wars in history.

5. Established international political-legal mechanisms have failed to prevent this attack and to hold the perpetrators accountable. The impunity that the U.S. government and its allies enjoy has created a serious international crisis that questions the import and significance of international law, of human rights covenants, and of the ability of international institutions including the United Nations to address the crisis with any degree of authority or dignity.

6. The U.S./UK occupation of Iraq of the last twenty-seven months has led to the destruction and devastation of the Iraqi state and society. Law and order have broken down, resulting in a pervasive lack of human security. The physical infrastructure is in shambles; the health care delivery system is in poor condition; the education system has virtually ceased to function; there is massive environmental and ecological devastation; and the cultural and archeological heritage of the Iraqi people has been desecrated.

7. The occupation has intentionally exacerbated ethnic, sectarian, and religious divisions in Iraqi society, with the aim of undermining Iraq's identity and integrity as a nation. This is in keeping with the familiar imperial policy of divide and rule. Moreover, it has facilitated rising levels of violence against women, increased gender oppression, and reinforced patriarchy.

8. The imposition of the UN sanctions in 1990 caused untold suffering and thousands of deaths. The situation has worsened after the occupation. At least one hundred thousand civilians have been killed; sixty thousand are being held in U.S. custody in inhumane conditions, without charges; thousands have disappeared; and torture has become routine.

9. The illegal privatization, deregulation, and liberalization of the Iraqi economy by the occupation regime has coerced the country into becoming a client economy that is controlled by the IMF and the World Bank, both of which are integral to the Washington Consensus. The occupying forces have also acquired control over Iraq's oil reserves.

10. Any law or institution created under the aegis of occupation is devoid of both legal and moral authority. The recently concluded election, the Constituent Assembly, the current government, and the drafting committee for the Constitution are therefore all illegitimate.

11. There is widespread opposition to the occupation. Political, social, and civil resistance through peaceful means is subjected to repression by the occupying forces. It is the occupation and its brutality that has provoked a strong armed resistance and certain acts of desperation. By the principles embodied in the UN Charter and in international law, the popular national resistance to the occupation is legitimate and justified. It deserves the support of people everywhere who care for justice and freedom.

II. CHARGES

On the basis of the preceding findings and recalling the Charter of the United Nations and other legal documents indicated in the appendix, the jury has established the following charges.

A. Against the Governments of the U.S. and the UK

1. Planning, preparing, and waging the supreme crime of a war of aggression in contravention of the United Nations Charter and the Nuremberg Principles.

Evidence for this can be found in the leaked Downing Street Memo of 23 July 2002, in which it was revealed: "Military action was now seen as inevitable. Bush wanted to remove Saddam through military action, justified by the conjunction of terrorism and WMD. But the intelligence and facts were being fixed around the policy." Intelligence was manufactured to willfully deceive the people of the U.S., the UK, and their elected representatives.

2. Targeting the civilian population of Iraq and civilian infrastructure by intentionally directing attacks upon civilians and hospitals, medical centers, residential neighborhoods, electricity stations, and water purification facilities. The complete destruction of the city of Falluja in itself constitutes a glaring example of such crimes.

3. Using disproportionate force and weapon systems with indiscriminate effects, such as cluster munitions, incendiary bombs, depleted uranium (DU), and chemical weapons. Detailed evidence was presented to the Tribunal by expert witnesses that leukemia had risen sharply in children under the age of five residing in those areas that had been targeted by DU weapons.

4. Using DU munitions in spite of all the warnings presented by scientists and war veterans on their devastating long-term effects on human beings and the environment. The U.S. Administration, claiming lack of scientifically established proof of the harmful effects of DU, decided to risk the lives of millions for several generations rather than discontinue its use on account of the potential risks. This alone displays the Administration's wanton disregard for human life. The Tribunal heard testimony concerning the current obstruction by the U.S. Administration of the efforts of Iraqi universities to collect data and conduct research on the issue.

5. Failing to safeguard the lives of civilians during military activi-

ties and during the occupation period thereafter. This is evidenced, for example, by "shock and awe" bombing techniques and the conduct of occupying forces at checkpoints.

6. Actively creating conditions under which the status of Iraqi women has seriously been degraded, contrary to the repeated claims of the leaders of the coalition forces. Women's freedom of movement has severely been limited, restricting their access to the public sphere, to education, livelihood, political and social engagement. Testimony was provided that sexual violence and sex trafficking have increased since the occupation of Iraq began.

7. Using deadly violence against peaceful protestors, including the April 2003 killing of more than a dozen peaceful protestors in Falluja.

8. Imposing punishments without charge or trial, including collective punishment, on the people of Iraq. Repeated testimonies pointed to "snatch and grab" operations, disappearances and assassinations.

9. Subjecting Iraqi soldiers and civilians to torture and cruel, inhuman, or degrading treatment. Degrading treatment includes subjecting Iraqi soldiers and civilians to acts of racial, ethnic, religious, and gender discrimination, as well as denying Iraqi soldiers Prisoner of War status as required by the Geneva Conventions. Abundant testimony was provided of unlawful arrests and detentions, without due process of law. Well known and egregious examples of torture and cruel and inhuman treatment occurred in Abu Ghraib prison as well as in Mosul, Camp Bucca, and Basra. The employment of mercenaries and private contractors to carry out torture has served to undermine accountability.

10. Rewriting the laws of a country that has been illegally invaded and occupied, in violation of international covenants on the

responsibilities of occupying powers, in order to amass illegal profits (through such measures as Order 39, signed by L. Paul Bremer III for the Coalition Provisional Authority, which allows foreign investors to buy and take over Iraq's state-owned enterprises and to repatriate 100 percent of their profits and assets at any point) and to control Iraq's oil. Evidence was presented of a number of corporations that had profited from such transactions.

11. Willfully devastating the environment, contaminating it by DU weapons, combined with the plumes from burning oil wells, as well as huge oil spills, and destroying agricultural lands. Deliberately disrupting the water and waste removal systems, in a manner verging on biological-chemical warfare. Failing to prevent the looting and dispersal of radioactive material from nuclear sites. Extensive documentation is available on air and water pollution, land degradation, and radioactive pollution.

12. Failing to protect humanity's rich archaeological and cultural heritage in Iraq by allowing the looting of museums and established historical sites and positioning military bases in culturally and archeologically sensitive locations. This took place despite prior warnings from UNESCO and Iraqi museum officials.

13. Obstructing the right to information, including the *censoring* of Iraqi media, such as newspapers (e.g., *al-Hawza, al-Mashriq* and *al-Mustaqila*) and radio stations (Baghdad Radio), the shutting down of the Baghdad offices of Al Jazeera Television, targeting international journalists, imprisoning and killing academics, intellectuals, and scientists.

14. Redefining torture in violation of international law to allow use of torture and illegal detentions, including holding more than five hundred people at Guantánamo Bay without charging them or allowing them any access to legal protection, and using "extraordi-

nary renditions" to send people to be tortured in other countries known to commit human rights abuses and torture prisoners.

15. Committing a crime against peace by violating the will of the global anti-war movement. In an unprecedented display of public conscience millions of people across the world stood in opposition to the imminent attack on Iraq. The attack rendered them effectively voiceless. This amounts to a declaration by the U.S. government and its allies to millions of people that their voices can be ignored, suppressed, and silenced with complete impunity.

16. Engaging in policies to wage permanent war on sovereign nations. Syria and Iran have already been declared as potential targets. In declaring a "global war on terror," the U.S. government has given itself the exclusive right to use aggressive military force against any target of its choosing. Ethnic and religious hostilities are being fueled in different parts of the world. The U.S. occupation of Iraq has further emboldened the Israeli occupation in Palestine and increased the repression of the Palestinian people. The focus on state security and the escalation of militarization has caused a serious deterioration of human security and civil rights across the world.

B. Against the Security Council of the United Nations

1. Failing to protect the Iraqi people against the crime of aggression.

2. Imposing harsh economic sanctions on Iraq, despite knowledge that sanctions were directly contributing to the massive loss of civilian lives and harming innocent civilians.

3. Allowing the United States and United Kingdom to carry out illegal bombings in the no-fly zones, using false pretenses of enforcing UN resolutions, and at no point allowing discussion in the Secu-

rity Council of this violation, and thereby being complicit and responsible for loss of civilian life and destruction of Iraqi infrastructure.

4. Allowing the United States to dominate the United Nations and hold itself above any accountability by other member nations.

5. Failure to stop war crimes and crimes against humanity by the United States and its coalition partners in Iraq.

6. Failure to hold the United States and its coalition partners accountable for violations of international law during the invasion and occupation, giving official sanction to the occupation and therefore, both by acts of commission and acts of omission, becoming a collaborator in an illegal occupation.

C. Against the Governments of the Coalition of the Willing

Collaborating in the invasion and occupation of Iraq, thus sharing responsibility in the crimes committed.

D. Against the Governments of Other Countries

Allowing the use of military bases and air space, and providing other logistical support, for the invasion and occupation, and hence being complicit in the crimes committed.

E. Against the Private Corporations Which Have Won Contracts for the Reconstruction of Iraq and Which Have Sued for and Received "Reparation Awards" from the Illegal Occupation Regime.

Profiting from the war with complicity in the crimes described above, of invasion and occupation.

F. Against the Major Corporate Media

1. Disseminating the deliberate falsehoods spread by the governments of the U.S. and the UK and failing to adequately investigate this misinformation, even in the face of abundant evidence to the contrary. Among the corporate media houses that bear special responsibility for promoting the lies about Iraq's weapons of mass destruction, we name the *New York Times,* in particular their reporter Judith Miller, whose main source was on the payroll of the CIA. We also name Fox News, CNN, NBC, CBS, ABC, the BBC, and ITN. This list also includes, but is not limited to, *The Express, The Sun, The Observer* and *The Washington Post.*

2. Failing to report the atrocities being committed against Iraqi people by the occupying forces, neglecting the duty to give privilege and dignity to voices of suffering, and marginalizing the global voices for peace and justice.

3. Failing to report fairly on the ongoing occupation; silencing and discrediting dissenting voices and failing to adequately report on the full national costs and consequences of the invasion and occupation of Iraq; disseminating the propaganda of the occupation regime that seeks to justify the continuation of its presence in Iraq on false grounds.

4. Inciting an ideological climate of fear, racism, xenophobia, and Islamophobia, which is then used to justify and legitimize violence perpetrated by the armies of the occupying regime.

5. Disseminating an ideology that glorifies masculinity and combat, while normalizing war as a policy choice.

6. Complicity in the waging of an aggressive war and perpetuating a regime of occupation that is widely regarded as guilty of war crimes and crimes against humanity.

7. Enabling, through the validation and dissemination of disinformation, the fraudulent misappropriation of human and financial resources for an illegal war waged on false pretexts.

8. Promoting corporate-military perspectives on "security" that are counter-productive to the fundamental concerns and priorities of the global population and have seriously endangered civilian populations.

III. RECOMMENDATIONS

Recognizing the right of the Iraqi people to resist the illegal occupation of their country and to develop independent institutions, and affirming that the right to resist the occupation is the right to wage a struggle for self-determination, freedom, and independence as derived from the Charter of the United Nations, we the Jury of Conscience declare our solidarity with the people of Iraq.

We recommend:

1. The immediate and unconditional withdrawal of the Coalition forces from Iraq.

2. That Coalition governments make war reparations and pay compensation to Iraq for the humanitarian, economic, ecological, and cultural devastation they have caused by their illegal invasion and occupation.

3. That all laws, contracts, treaties, and institutions established under occupation, which the Iraqi people deem inimical to their interests, be considered null and void.

4. That the Guantánamo Bay prison and all other offshore U.S. military prisons be closed immediately, that the names of the prisoners be disclosed, that they receive POW status, and receive due process.

5. That there be an exhaustive investigation of those responsible for the crime of aggression, war crimes, and crimes against humanity in Iraq, beginning with George W. Bush, President of the United States of America, Tony Blair, Prime Minister of the United Kingdom, those in key decision-making positions in these countries and in the Coalition of the Willing, those in the military chain-of-command who masterminded the strategy for and carried out this criminal war, starting from the very top and going down; as well as personalities in Iraq who helped prepare this illegal invasion and supported the occupiers.

We list some of the most obvious names to be included in such investigation: prime ministers of the Coalition of the Willing, such as Junichiro Koizumi of Japan, José María Aznar of Spain, Silvio Berlusconi of Italy, José Manuel Durão Barroso and Santana Lopes of Portugal, Roh Moo Hyun of South Korea, Anders Fogh Rasmussen of Denmark; public officials such as Dick Cheney, Donald H. Rumsfeld, Paul Wolfowitz, Colin L. Powell, Condoleezza Rice, Richard Perle, Douglas Feith, Alberto Gonzales, L. Paul Bremer from the U.S., and Jack Straw, Geoffrey Hoon, John Reid, Adam Ingram from the UK; military commanders beginning with: Gen. Richard Myers, Gen. Tommy Franks, Gen. John P. Abizaid, Gen. Ricardo S. Sanchez, Gen. Thomas Metz, Gen. John R. Vines, Gen. George Casey from the U.S.; Gen. Mike Jackson, Gen. John Kiszely, Air Marshal Brian Burridge, Gen. Peter Wall, Rear Admiral David Snelson, Gen. Robin Brims, Air Vice-Marshal Glenn Torpy from the UK; and chiefs of staff and commanding officers of all coalition countries with troops in Iraq; Iraqi collaborators such as Ahmed Chalabi, Iyad Allawi, Abdul Aziz Al Hakim, and Gen. Abdul Qader Mohammed Jassem Mohan, among others.

6. That a process of accountability is initiated to hold those

morally and personally responsible for their participation in this illegal war, such as journalists who deliberately lied, corporate media outlets that promoted racial, ethnic, and religious hatred, and CEOs of multinational corporations that profited from this war.

7. That people throughout the world launch nonviolent actions against U.S. and UK corporations that directly profit from this war. Examples of such corporations include Halliburton, Bechtel, The Carlyle Group, CACI Inc., Titan Corporation, Kellogg, Brown & Root (subsidiary of Halliburton), DynCorp, Boeing, ExxonMobil, Texaco, British Petroleum. The following companies have sued Iraq and received "reparation awards": Toys "Я" Us, Kentucky Fried Chicken, Shell, Nestlé, Pepsi, Phillip Morris, Sheraton, Mobil. Such actions may take the form of direct actions such as shutting down their offices, consumer boycotts, and pressure on shareholders to divest.

8. That young people and soldiers act on conscientious objection and refuse to enlist and participate in an illegal war. Also, that countries provide conscientious objectors with political asylum.

9. That the international campaign for dismantling all U.S. military bases abroad be reinforced.

10. That people around the world resist and reject any effort by any of their governments to provide material, logistical, or moral support to the occupation of Iraq.

We, the Jury of Conscience, hope that the scope and specificity of these recommendations will lay the groundwork for a world in which international institutions will be shaped and reshaped by the will of people and not by fear and self-interest, where journalists and intellectuals will not remain mute, where the will of the people of the world will be central, and human security will prevail over state security and corporate profits.

Arundhati Roy, India, Spokesperson of the Jury of Conscience
Ahmet Öztürk, Turkey
Ayşe Erzan, Turkey
Chandra Muzaffar, Malaysia
David Krieger, United States
Eve Ensler, United States
François Houtart, Belgium
Jae-Bok Kim, South Korea
Mehmet Tarhan, Turkey
Miguel Angel De Los Santos Cruz, Mexico
Murat Belge, Turkey
Rela Mazali, Israel
Salaam Al Jobourie, Iraq
Taty Almeida, Argentina

ACKNOWLEDGMENTS

THANKS TO: Howard Zinn; Colin Robinson, a friend and a brilliant publisher, who first encouraged me to write this book (which I hoped someone else might undertake) and whose support and editing have been invaluable; Elizabeth Seidlin-Bernstein, Sarah Fan, Ina Howard, Ellen Adler, and the New Press staff for all their work on this project; J. Patrick Lannan Jr., Jaune Evans, Linda Carey, and the staff of the Lannan Foundation, who provided the very supportive environment in which I wrote the first draft of this book; Jessie Kindig, for her invaluable research assistance; Askold Melnyczuk, Omar Waraich, and David Whitehouse for help with additional references; Brenda Coughlin, Dahr Jamail, Jeff Guntzel, Lance Selfa, Lily Thorne, Paul D'Amato, Phil Gasper, and Shea Dean, who provided very useful critical feedback on the manuscript; Christian Parenti, for his thoughtful comments during and after a work-in-progress discussion organized by Sasheem Silkiss-Hero; Aja Shevelew, for her meticulous copyedit, and Kelly Farley and Monica Hopkins of dix! for first-rate production assistance; John E. Pike for help with the figures on coalition troop levels in Iraq; Julie Fain and David Whitehouse, for help with the map of Iraq and index, and Craig Remington and the University of Alabama map collection for permission to use their base map; Ayça Çubukçu and all my kind hosts at the World Tribunal on Iraq in Istanbul; Arundhati Roy; my many comrades at Haymarket Books, *International Socialist Review,* and the International Socialist Organization; and B.C.C., without whom it wouldn't ring true.

NOTES

I HAVE RELIED as often as possible on accessible, mainstream news sources in writing this book, so that readers can easily verify my citations. In checking these references, keep in mind that articles sometimes appear on different pages and under different headlines in various national and regional editions of major newspapers. An article in the London edition of the *Financial Times* may appear on a different page and with a different title (or even byline, in some cases) than the one in the edition I read in Brooklyn (just as the *New York Times* is not the same in California as it is in New York). That same *Financial Times* article may appear in Lexis-Nexis archives under another title. In addition, for newspaper articles, my citation is to the first page on which an article begins, though in some cases the actual material I am citing comes from material on a page to which the article jumps. In the case of long articles in supplements, such as the *New York Times Magazine,* I provide the page number on which the material I am citing actually appears.

Many of the articles I have cited here are readily available on the Internet. To avoid further cluttering the notes, I generally provide web references only to articles that appear exclusively online or that might be otherwise difficult to locate. Web references are problematic for two reasons, however: many people still do not have regular access to the Internet, and web links change regularly and can be quite unreliable (as can much information that passes as "fact" on the Internet).

FOREWORD

1. Editorial, "Grim Realities in Iraq," *New York Times*, December 22, 2004, p. A30.
2. Howard Zinn, *Vietnam: The Logic of Withdrawal* (Boston: Beacon Press, 1967; Cambridge: South End Press, 2002).

INTRODUCTION

1. Howard Zinn, *Vietnam: The Logic of Withdrawal* (Boston: Beacon Press, 1967; Cambridge: South End Press, 2002).
2. Richard Cohen, "Vietnam It Isn't," *Washington Post*, October 30, 2003, p. A23.
3. Caroline Daniel and Guy Dinmore, "McCain Calls for 10,000 More Iraq Troops," *Financial Times* (London), November 11, 2005, p. 12.
4. See Philip Jones Griffiths, *Agent Orange: "Collateral Damage" in Viet Nam* (London: Trolley Ltd., 2003).
5. Andrew Metz, "Bridging the Chemical Divide," *Newsday*, August 1, 2005, p. A18. See also Andrew Metz, "Opening a Closing Door," *Newsday*, July 31, 2005, p. A36. William Glaberson, "Civil Lawsuit on Defoliant in Vietnam Is Dismissed," *New York Times*, March 1, 2005, p. B6.
6. William Glaberson, "U.S. Urges Judge to Dismiss Suit on Agent Orange Use in Vietnam," *New York Times*, February 28, 2005, p. B3.
7. See Elaine C. Hagopian, ed., *Civil Rights in Peril: The Targeting of Arabs and Muslims* (Chicago: Haymarket Books, 2004); Rachel Meeropol, ed., *America's Disappeared: Secret Imprisonment, Detainees, and the "War on Terror"* (New York: Seven Stories Press/Open Media, 2004);

David Cole, *Enemy Aliens: Double Standards and Constitutional Freedoms in the War on Terrorism* (New York: The New Press, 2003); Michael Ratner and Ellen Ray, *Guantánamo: What the World Should Know* (White River Junction, Vermont: Chelsea Green, 2004); David Rose, *Guantánamo: The War on Human Rights* (New York: The New Press, 2004); Mark Dow, *American Gulag: Inside U.S. Immigration Prisons* (Berkeley: University of California Press, 2004); Karen J. Greenberg and Joshua L. Dratel, eds., *The Torture Papers: The Road to Abu Ghraib* (Cambridge: Cambridge University Press, 2005); and Alfred W. McCoy, *A Question of Torture: CIA Interrogation, from the Cold War to the War on Terror* (New York: Metropolitan Books/Henry Holt, 2006).

8. Tim Golden and Eric Schmitt, "Detainee Policy Sharply Divides Bush Officials," *New York Times,* November 2, 2005, p. A1. See also David Cole, "What Bush Wants to Hear," *New York Review of Books* 52, no. 18 (November 17, 2005), pp. 8–12.

9. Daniel Dombey, James Bosell, and Steve Negus, "US Warned on Long Presence in Iraq as Constitution Approved by Slim Majority," *Financial Times* (London), October 26, 2005, p. 1. Stephen Fidler, "Steady Growth Expected After the Bubble," *Financial Times* (London), September 13, 2005, "Defence Industry," special report, p. 4.

10. Stephen Fidler, "Operating in a Troubling Legal and Regulatory Vacuum," *Financial Times* (London), May 9, 2005, "Worldwide Security," special report, p. 2. Felix Rohatyn and Allison Stanger, "The Profit Motive Goes to War," *Financial Times* (London), November 17, 2004, p. 19.

11. Chart based on Global Security.org data, compiled from news sources (available at http://www.globalsecurity.org/military/ops/iraq_orbat_coalition.htm), Reuters, "Who's Leaving Iraq?" *Christian Science Monitor,* April 13, 2005, p. 11, and Associated Press, "Countries Contributing Forces to U.S.-led Coalition in Iraq," December 1, 2005. See also Sarah Anderson, Phyllis Bennis, and John Cavanagh, *Coalition of the Willing or Coalition of the Coerced?: How the Bush Administration Influences Allies in Its War on Iraq* (Washington, D.C.: Institute for Policy Studies,

2003). Fiji entered Iraq as part of the UN Assistance Mission in Iraq; Hungary entered as part of the NATO Training Force; Singapore sent a landing ship to Iraq, which returned in March 2005; other countries provided air and base support. While the Netherlands withdrew the bulk of its troops, nineteen remained in Iraq at the end of 2005.

1. A WAR OF CHOICE

1. The Editors, "The *Times* and Iraq," *New York Times,* May 26, 2004, p. 10.
2. See Amy Goodman and David Goodman, *The Exception to the Rulers: Exposing Oily Politicians, War Profiteers, and the Media That Love Them* (New York: Hyperion, 2004), pp. 137–47.
3. Howard Kurtz, "Prewar Articles Questioning Threat Often Didn't Make Front Page," *Washington Post,* August 12, 2004, p. A1.
4. Ibid.
5. Ibid.
6. Bruce Anderson, "Everyone Should Now Agree: The Worst Thing for the Iraqis Would Be an American Defeat," *The Independent* (London), April 12, 2004, p. 25.
7. See, among other examples, Thomas L. Friedman, "Fire, Ready, Aim," *New York Times,* March 9, 2003, sec. 4, p. 1.
8. Jeffrey Goldberg, "A Little Learning: What Douglas Feith Knew and When He Knew It," *New Yorker,* May 9, 2005, p. 39.
9. Nicholas Lemann, "The Next World Order," *New Yorker,* April 1, 2002, p. 44.
10. See, among many other articles, Joe Battenfield, "Americans Buck Bush on Attacking Iraq," *Boston Herald,* September 4, 2002, p. 1, and Dana Milbank and Claudia Deane, "Hussein Link to 9/11 Lingers in Many Minds," *Washington Post,* September 6, 2003, p. A1.
11. "I'm a war president. I make decisions here in the Oval Office in foreign-policy matters with war on my mind," Bush told Tim Russert in an hour-long interview. President George W. Bush, interview with Tim

Russert, *Meet the Press,* NBC, February 8, 2005. See also Frank Rich, "Karl and Scooter's Excellent Adventure," *New York Times,* October 23, 2005, sec. 4, p. 13. For a detailed analysis of the selling of the war, see John Prados, *Hoodwinked: The Documents That Reveal How Bush Sold Us a War* (New York: The New Press, 2004). See also Norman Solomon, *War Made Easy: How Presidents and Pundits Keep Spinning Us to Death* (Hoboken, New Jersey: John Wiley & Sons, 2005).

12. William Kristol, the editor of the *Weekly Standard* magazine, quoted in Guy Dunmore, "Ideologues Reshape World over Breakfast," *Financial Times* (London), March 22, 2003, p. 1.

13. David M. Shribman, "The Disappearing Bully Pulpit," *Boston Globe Magazine,* April 20, 1997, p. 17.

14. George Packer, "Dreaming of Democracy," *New York Times Magazine,* March 2, 2003, sec. 7, p. 49.

15. Carola Hoyos, "Baghdad Re-entry to Market 'Could Have Big Impact,' " *Financial Times* (London), February 21, 2003, p. 3.

16. Simon Romero, "Demand for Natural Gas Brings Big Import Plans, and Objections," *New York Times,* June 15, 2005, p. A1.

17. Some critics of the Iraq war have argued that the Bush administration was driven to invade Iraq by fear that Saddam Hussein would lead a trend toward denominating oil purchases in euros, the currency of the twelve-nation European Union, rather than U.S. dollars. Though the United States does derive benefits from dollar-based oil trading, and even more so from the dollar being the leading reserve currency of the world, the real prize for the United States is not the denomination of world oil transactions in dollars, but control of oil and the geostrategic advantages that flow from this. For a fuller development of this argument, see Anthony Arnove, review of Research Unit for Political Economy, *Behind the Invasion of Iraq* (New York: Monthly Review Press, 2002), in *International Socialist Review* 32 (November–December 2003), p. 83.

18. Thomas Catan and David Ibison, "Libya Opens Up Its Oil to Asia and

Europe," *Financial Times* (London), October 4, 2005, p. 32. Ken Belson, "Why Japan Steps Gingerly in the Middle East," *New York Times*, September 17, 2002, p. W1. For detailed data on U.S. oil imports, see Energy Information Administration (Department of Energy), Supplemental Tables to the *Annual Energy Outlook 2005*, Table 117, Imported Petroleum by Source. Available online at http://www.eia.doe.gov/oiaf/aeo/supplement/supref.html. In this calculation, the category of Middle East excludes North African oil. Including North African oil raises the figure to closer to 15 percent for 2004. See also Michael Klare, "Resources," in John Feffer, ed., *Power Trip: U.S. Unilateralism and Global Strategy After September 11* (New York: Seven Stories Press, 2003), pp. 53–55.

19. Keith Bradsher, "2 Big Appetites Take Seats at the Oil Table," *New York Times*, February 18, 2005, p. C1.

20. Michael Klare, "For Oil and Empire? Rethinking War with Iraq," *Current History* 102, no. 662 (March 2003), p. 134. See also Klare, "U.N. Charade: Timing of Iraq War in Bush's Hands from Start," Pacific News Service, February 12, 2003.

21. Michael Klare, "The Carter Doctrine Goes Global," *The Progressive*, December 2004, p. 18. See also Michael Klare, *Blood and Oil: The Dangers and Consequences of America's Growing Petroleum Dependency* (New York: Owl Books/Henry Holt, 2005). Carter enunciated the doctrine in his 1980 State of the Union address. "Quotation of the Day," *New York Times*, January 24, 1980, sec. 2, p. 1.

22. Klare, "The Carter Doctrine Goes Global," p. 17.

23. Hoyos, "Baghdad Re-entry to Market," p. 3.

24. Quoted in Packer, "Dreaming of Democracy," sec. 7, p. 49.

25. David E. Sanger and James Dao, "U.S. Is Completing Plan to Promote a Democratic Iraq," *New York Times*, January 6, 2003, p. A1.

26. Neela Bannerjee, "Army Depots in Iraqi Desert Have Names of Oil Giants," *New York Times*, March 27, 2003, p. C14. See also Richard Sisk, "U.S. Battle Plan: Slip In and Grab Oil Fields," *Daily News* (New York), January 23, 2003, p. 7.

27. Robert Fisk, "Americans Defend Two Untouchable Ministries from the Hordes of Looters," *The Independent* (London), April 14, 2003, p. 7. Patrick E. Tyler, "Barrels Looted from Nuclear Site Raise Fears for Villagers in Iraq," *New York Times,* June 8, 2003, sec. 1, p. 1.

28. Richard W. Stevenson and David E. Sanger, "Calling Iraq a Serious Threat, Bush Vows That He'll Disarm It, and Also Rebuild U.S. Economy," *New York Times,* January 29, 2003, p. A1.

29. Anthony Shadid, "Iraqi Tribunal Calls Top Hussein Aide," *Washington Post,* December 19, 2004, p. A32.

30. Elaine Sciolino, "Shultz to See Iraqi on Reported Gassing of Kurds," *New York Times,* September 8, 1988, p. A16.

31. Clifford Krauss, "Bush Aide Opposes Sanctions on Iraq," *New York Times,* June 16, 1990, sec. 1, p. 3.

32. Jim Hoagland, "Atrocity Du Jour," *Washington Post,* March 26, 1988, p. A2.

33. Gary Thatcher and Timothy Aeppel, "The Trail to Samarra," *Christian Science Monitor,* December 13, 1988, p. B1.

34. Sciolino, "Shultz to See Iraqi on Reported Gassing of Kurds," p. A16.

35. Amy Kaslow, "US Eyes Sanctions Against Iraq," *Christian Science Monitor,* August 31, 1989, p. 9.

36. Michael Kranish, "Invasion Changed Views of Five Senators Who Met Hussein," *Boston Globe,* August 12, 1990, p. 23.

37. "From a marketing point of view," Card said, "you don't introduce new products in August." Quoted in Elisabeth Bumiller, "Bush Aides Set Strategy to Sell Policy on Iraq," *New York Times,* September 7, 2002, p. A1. For more on the public relations campaign to sell the war, specifically the role of the Rendon Group, see James Bamford, "The Man Who Sold the War," *Rolling Stone,* December 1, 2005, pp. 53–62.

38. Secretary of State Colin Powell, Remarks in Egypt with Egyptian Foreign Minister Amre Moussa, February 24, 2001. Quoted in John Pilger, "The Big Lie," *Daily Mirror* (London), September 22, 2003, p. 6. See also Pilger's excellent film *Breaking the Silence: Truth and Lies in the War on Terror* (Oley, Pennsylvania: Bullfrog Films, 2003).

39. National Security Adviser Condoleezza Rice, interview with John King, *Late Edition with Wolf Blitzer*, CNN, July 29, 2001. Quoted in Pilger, "The Big Lie," p. 6.

40. Michael Smith, "The Real News in the Downing Street Memos," *Los Angeles Times*, June 23, 2005, p. B13. For excellent information on the British propaganda campaign and its consequences, see Mark Curtis, *Unpeople: Britain's Secret Human Rights Abuses* (London: Vintage, 2004), part I and part II.

41. Quoted in Maureen Dowd, "Desert Spring, Sprung," *New York Times*, March 9, 2003, sec. 4, p. 15.

2. THE REALITY OF OCCUPATION

1. Pentagon planners took the phrase from Harlan K. Ullman and James P. Wade, *Shock and Awe: Achieving Rapid Dominance* (Washington, D.C.: Center for Advanced Concepts and Technology, 1996).

2. For documentation on the United Nations study and the impact of the sanctions more generally, see Anthony Arnove, ed., *Iraq Under Siege: The Deadly Impact of Sanctions and War*, 2nd ed. (Cambridge: South End Press; London: Pluto Press, 2003).

3. Stephen Kinzer, "Smart Bombs, Dumb Sanctions," *New York Times*, January 3, 1999, sec. 4, p. 4. See also Joy Gordon, "Cool War: Economic Sanctions as a Weapon of Mass Destruction," *Harper's* (November 2002), pp. 43–49. For a personal account, see Anthony Arnove, "Scenes from Iraq," *Agni*, no. 54 (2001), pp. 34–42.

4. James Glanz, "Iraqis Simmer as Demand Outstrips Electricity Supply," *New York Times*, July 23, 2005, p. A5. See also T. Christian Miller, "Some Iraq Projects Running Out of Money, U.S. Says," *Los Angeles Times*, September 8, 2005, p. A6.

5. Howard LaFranchi, "Goodwill Is Fragile in New Iraq," *Christian Science Monitor*, November 5, 2003, p. 1.

6. Glanz, "Iraqis Simmer as Demand Outstrips Electricity Supply," p. A5.

7. Rick Jervis, "Iraq Rebuilding Slows as U.S. Money for Projects Dries Up," *USA Today,* October 10, 2005, p. 1A.

8. Public Citizen, with Dahr Jamail, *Bechtel's Dry Run: Iraqis Suffer Water Crisis* (April 2004), p. 3. Available online at http://dahrjamailiraq .com/reports/.

9. Jeffrey Gettleman, "Chaos and War Leave Iraq's Hospitals in Ruins," *New York Times,* February 14, 2004, p. A1.

10. Dahr Jamail, *Iraqi Hospitals Ailing Under Occupation* (June 21, 2005), p. 3. Available online at http://dahrjamailiraq.com/reports/.

11. Ibid., p. 34.

12. Michael R. Gordon, "Debate Lingering on Decision to Dissolve the Iraqi Military," *New York Times,* October 21, 2004, p. A1. Matthew Fisher, "U.S. Admits Error, Welcomes Baathists," *Ottawa Citizen,* April 24, 2004, p. A9.

13. Jonathan Finer and Omar Fekeiki, "Tackling Another Major Challenge in Iraq: Unemployment," *Washington Post,* June 20, 2005, p. A10.

14. Bryan Bender, "U.S. Hiring Goals Fall Far Short in Reconstruction," *Boston Globe,* July 11, 2004, p. A6.

15. Christian Parenti, *The Freedom: Shadows and Hallucinations in Occupied Iraq* (New York: The New Press, 2004), p. 206.

16. T. Christian Miller, "Some Iraq Projects Running Out of Money, U.S. Says," *Los Angeles Times,* September 8, 2005, p. A6. T. Christian Miller, "U.S. Officials Suspected of Embezzlement in Iraq," *Los Angeles Times,* May 5, 2005, p. A5.

17. Antonia Juhasz, "Bush's Economic Invasion of Iraq," *Los Angeles Times,* August 14, 2005, p. M5. See also Antonia Juhasz, *The Bush Agenda: Invading the World One Economy at a Time* (New York: Regan Books, 2006) and Ed Harriman, "Where Has All the Money Gone?" *London Review of Books* 27, no. 13 (July 7, 2005), pp. 3–7.

18. Tariq Ali, *Bush in Babylon: The Recolonisation of Iraq,* 2nd ed. (New York: Verso, 2004), p. 3.

19. David Bacon, "Saddam's Labor Laws Live On," *The Progressive* (Decem-

ber 2003), pp. 20–23. Herbert Docena, " 'Shock and Awe' Therapy," presentation at the World Tribunal on Iraq, Istanbul, Turkey, June 25, 2005. Available online at http://www.worldtribunal.org/main/popup/docena.doc.

20. Neil King Jr., "Bush Officials Draft Broad Plan For Free-Market Economy in Iraq," *Wall Street Journal,* May 1, 2003, p. A1.

21. Jeff Madrick, "The Economic Plan for Iraq Seems Long on Ideology, Short on Common Sense," *New York Times,* October 2, 2003, p. C2.

22. Naomi Klein, "Baghdad Year Zero," *Harper's* (September 2004), p. 44.

23. For a powerful personal account, see Riverbend, *Baghdad Burning: Girl Blog from Iraq* (New York: The Feminist Press, 2005).

24. Dexter Filkins, "The Fall of the Warrior King," *New York Times Magazine,* October 23, 2005, sec. 6, p. 57.

25. Ibid., sec. 6, p. 59.

26. Antonio Castaneda, "Iraqis Forced to Take in Uninvited Troops," Associated Press, October 27, 2005.

27. Bradley Graham, "Over Iraq, Pilots Fly Into Action When Troops Call for Help," *Washington Post,* December 19, 2004, p. A31.

28. The Declaration of Independence, July 4, 1776. Transcript and facsimile available on the web site of the U.S. National Archives and Records Administration (http://www.archives.gov).

29. Kirk Semple and Edward Wong, "Major Offensive Hits Insurgents on Iraqi Border," *New York Times,* November 6, 2005, sec. 1, p. 1.

30. Francis Williams, "Most Detainees in Iraq Arrested by Mistake, Says Red Cross," *Financial Times* (London), May 11, 2004, p. 10.

31. Ibid.

32. Ibid.

33. Eric Schmitt, "3 in 82nd Airborne Say Beating Iraqi Prisoners Was Routine," *New York Times,* September 24, 2005, p. A1. Human Rights Watch, *Leadership Failure: Firsthand Accounts of Torture of Iraqi Detainees by the U.S. Army's 82nd Airborne Division,* vol. 17, no. 3(G), September 2005, available online at http://hrw.org/reports/2005/us0905/index.htm, and excerpted in "Torture in Iraq: A Report by

Human Rights Watch," *New York Review of Books* 52, no. 17 (November 3, 2005), pp. 67–72.

34. Ian Fisher, "Iraqi Recounts Hours of Abuse by U.S. Troops," *New York Times,* May 5, 2004, p. A1.

35. Edward Epstein, "Rumsfeld Warns of Photos Depicting Worse Abuses," *San Francisco Chronicles,* May 8, 2004, p. A1.

36. Mike Allen, "Bush Defends Year-Ago Claim of End of 'Major Combat' in Iraq," *Washington Post,* May 1, 2004, p. A7.

37. Seymour M. Hersh, "Torture at Abu Ghraib," *New Yorker,* May 10, 2004, p. 43.

38. International Committee of the Red Cross, *Report of the International Committee of the Red Cross (ICRC) on the Treatment by the Coalition Forces of Prisoners of War and Other Protected Persons by the Geneva Conventions in Iraq During Arrest, Internment and Interrogation* (February 2004). See excerpts in *The Guardian* (London), May 8, 2004, p. 4.

39. Quoted in Hendrik Hertzberg, "Unconventional War," *New Yorker,* May 24, 2004, p. 31.

40. Sewell Chan and Michael Amon, "Prisoner Abuse Probe Widened," *Washington Post,* May 2, 2004, p. A1.

41. Seymour M. Hersh, "Chain of Command: How the Department of Defense Mishandled the Disaster at Abu Ghraib," *New Yorker,* May 17, 2004, pp. 39–40.

42. Gary Younge and Julian Borger, "CBS Delayed Report on Iraqi Prison Abuse after Military Chiefs Plea," *The Guardian* (London), May 4, 2004, p. 4.

43. Jane Mayer, "Outsourcing Torture," *New Yorker,* February 14, 2005, p. 107. Michael Isikoff, "Secret Memo—Send to Be Tortured," *Newsweek,* August 8, 2005, p. 7. Kenneth Roth, "Terrorism Suspects Need to Be Prosecuted Not Tortured," *Financial Times,* November 21, 2005, p. 13.

44. Dana Priest, "CIA Holds Terror Suspects in Secret Prisons," *Washington Post,* November 2, 2005, p. A1. The article notes that *"The Washington Post* is not publishing the names of the Eastern European countries involved in the covert program, at the request of senior U.S. officials."

Human Rights Watch said that Poland and Romania are the most likely locations of the Eastern European secret detention centers. See Jan Cienski, Christopher Condon, Caroline Daniel, Guy Dinmore, Andrei Postelnicu, and Demetri Sevastopulo, "Evidence CIA Has Secret Jails in Europe," *Financial Times* (London), November 3, 2005, p. 1.

45. Douglass Jehl, Eric Schmitt, and Neil A. Lewis, "U.S. Military Says 26 Inmate Deaths May Be Homicide," *New York Times,* March 16, 2005, p. A1.

46. Douglas Jehl and Tim Golden, "C.I.A. Is Likely to Avoid Charges in Most Prisoner Deaths," *New York Times,* October 23, 2005, sec. 1, p. 6.

47. Dana Priest and Barton Gellman, "U.S. Decries Abuse but Defends Interrogations," *Washington Post,* December 26, 2002, p. A1. For the relevant background, see Naomi Klein, " 'Never Before': Our Amnesiac Torture Debate," *The Nation,* December 26, 2005, pp. 11–12; and Greg Grandin, *Empire's Workshop: Latin America and the Roots of U.S. Imperialism* (New York: Metropolitan Books/Henry Holt, 2006).

48. Ibid.

49. James Risen, David Johnston, and Neil A. Lewis, "Harsh C.I.A. Methods Cited in Top Qaeda Interrogations," *New York Times,* May 13, 2004, p. A1.

50. Jess Bravin, "Interrogation School Tells Army Recruits How Grilling Works—30 Techniques in 16 Weeks, Just Short of Torture," *Wall Street Journal,* April 26, 2002, p. A1.

51. Ibid.

52. Amnesty International, *Guantánamo and Beyond: The Continuing Pursuit of Unchecked Executive Power* (AI Index: AMR 51/063/2005), May 13, 2005. See also Peter Rothberg, "Gitmo's Shame," The Nation.com, October 4, 2005. Available at http://www.thenation.com/.

53. Bob Herbert, "Stories from the Inside," *New York Times,* February 7, 2005, p. A21.

54. Charlie Savage, "Detainees Attempted to Hang Selves," *Boston Globe,* January 25, 2005, p. A1.

55. Human Rights Watch, *Leadership Failure: Firsthand Accounts of Torture*

of Iraqi Detainees by the U.S. Army's 82nd Airborne Division, vol. 17, no. 3(G), September 2005. Human Rights Watch, "New Accounts of Torture by U.S. Troops," Press Release, September 24, 2005. See also Doug Struck, "Torture in Iraq Still Routine, Report Says," *Washington Post,* January 25, 2005, p. A1, and Josh White, "New Reports Surface about Detainee Abuse," *Washington Post,* September 24, 2005, p. A1.

56. Eric Schmitt and Thom Shanker, "U.S. Citing Abuse in Iraqi Prisons, Holds Detainees," *New York Times,* December 25, 2005, sec. 1, p. 1, and chart, sec. 1, p. 12. See also "The File: Prison Abuse," *San Francisco Chronicle,* June 20, 2004, p. 17.

57. Richard A. Oppel Jr., "Early Target of Offensive Is a Hospital," *New York Times,* November 8, 2004, p. A1. See also the accompanying photography by Shawn Baldwin.

58. Ibid.

59. Michael Jonofsky, "Rights Experts See Possibility of a War Crime," *New York Times,* November 13, 2004, p. A8.

60. Ali Fadhil, "City of Ghosts," *The Guardian* (London), January 11, 2005, sec. G2, p. 2.

61. "Excess deaths" is a calculation based on projections of current trends in population rates. In this case, *The Lancet* concluded that some Iraqis were not born who otherwise might have been had pre-occupation population trends continued, in addition to those who died prematurely or were killed as a result of the broad social consequences of the occupation. Les Roberts, Riyadh Lafta, Richard Garfield, Jamal Khudhairi, and Gilbert Burnham, "Mortality Before and After the 2003 Invasion of Iraq: Cluster Sample Survey," *The Lancet* 364, no. 9448 (November 20, 2004). See also the comment on the report by Richard Horton, "The War in Iraq: Civilian Casualties, Political Responsibilities," *The Lancet* 364, no. 9448 (November 20, 2004). For an excellent summary of the report, listen to Ira Glass, "What's in a Number?" *This American Life,* WBEZ Radio/Public Radio International, episode 300 (October 28, 2005), "Act One: Truth, Damn Truth, and Statistics" (audio available online at http://www.thislife.org/). See also Lila Guter-

man, "Researchers Who Rushed Into Print a Study of Iraqi Civilian Deaths Now Wonder Why It Was Ignored," *Chronicle of Higher Education,* January 27, 2005 (available online at http://chronicle.com/free/2005/01/2005012701n.htm).

62. Roberts et al., "Mortality Before and After the 2003 Invasion of Iraq: Cluster Sample Survey."

63. Hassan M. Fattah, "Civilian Toll in Iraq Is Placed at Nearly 25,000," *New York Times,* July 20, 2005, p. A8. By October 26, 2005, the *New York Times* reported, Iraq Body Count had put the number of Iraqi civilian deaths at 26,690 to 30,051, of whom 10 percent were children (Sabrina Tavernise, "Rising Civilian Toll Is the Iraq War's Silent, Sinister Pulse," *New York Times,* October 26, 2005, p. A12). See also Iraq Body Count, *A Dossier of Civilian Casualties 2003–2005* (July 2005) and the updated database on the Iraq Body Count web site: http://www.iraqbodycount.net/. In October 2005, the Pentagon for the first time reported on the deaths of Iraqi civilians and security personnel, but only those killed by insurgents. "No figures were provided for the number of Iraqis killed by American-led forces" (Sabrina Tavernise, "U.S. Quietly Issues Estimate of Iraqi Civilian Casualties," *New York Times,* October 30, 2005, sec. 1, p. 10).

64. Lila Guterman, "Dead Iraqis: Why an Estimate Was Ignored," *Columbia Journalism Review,* March–April 2005, p. 11.

65. Cesar G. Soriano and Steven Komarow, "Poll: Iraqis Losing Patience," *USA Today,* April 29, 2004, p. 1A. For more poll data, see Carl Conetta, *Vicious Circle: The Dynamics of Occupation and Resistance in Iraq, Part One: Patterns of Popular Discontent* (Project on Defense Alternatives Research Monograph No. 10), May 18, 2005, as well as Oxford Research International, National Survey of Iraq, June 2004.

66. Independent Institute for Administration and Civil Society Studies (IIACSS), *Public Opinion in Iraq: First Poll Following Abu Ghraib Revelations* (June 15, 2004), p. 35. Poll conducted May 14–23, 2004, in Baghdad, Baqubah, Basra, Diwaniyah, Hilla, and Mosul.

67. Ibid., p. 13.

68. Irene Sege, " 'Something Happened to Jeff,' " *Boston Globe,* March 1, 2005, p. E1. See also Charles W. Hoge et al., "Combat Duty in Iraq and Afghanistan, Mental Health Problems, and Barriers to Care," *New England Journal of Medicine* 351, no. 1 (July 1, 2004), pp. 13–22.

69. Interview with Amy Goodman, *Democracy Now!,* March 15, 2005.

3. THE NEW WHITE MAN'S BURDEN

1. Francis Fukuyama, "The Bush Doctrine, Before and After," *Financial Times* (London), October 11, 2005, p. 21.

2. Sidney Lens, *The Forging of the American Empire,* 2nd ed. (Chicago: Haymarket Books, 2004), p. 1. See also the introduction to the 2004 edition by Howard Zinn.

3. President George W. Bush, Commencement Address at West Point Military Academy, West Point, New York, June 1, 2002.

4. President George W. Bush, Remarks in Honor of Veterans Day, Washington, D.C., November 11, 2002.

5. Lens, *The Forging of the American Empire,* pp. 1–2.

6. Ibid., p. 14.

7. Ibid.

8. John O'Sullivan, "The Sun Set on One, but It Rises on Another," *Wall Street Journal,* April 10, 2003, p. D8, reviewing Niall Ferguson, *Empire: The Rise and Demise of the British World Order and the Lessons for Global Power* (New York: Basic Books, 2003). See also Niall Ferguson, *Colossus: The Rise and Fall of the American Empire* (New York: Penguin, 2004).

9. It is worth quoting Kipling's 1899 poem in full:

Take up the White Man's burden—
Send forth the best ye breed—
    Go bind your sons to exile
    To serve your captives' need;
To wait in heavy harness,
    On fluttered folk and wild—

Your new-caught, sullen peoples,
  Half devil and half child.

Take up the White Man's burden—
  In patience to abide,
To veil the threat of terror
  And check the show of pride;
By open speech and simple,
  An hundred times made plain,
To seek another's profit,
  And work another's gain.

Take up the White Man's burden—
  The savage wars of peace—
Fill full the mouth of Famine
  And bid the sickness cease;
And when your goal is nearest
  The end for others sought,
Watch Sloth and heathen Folly
  Bring all your hope to nought.

Take up the White Man's burden—
  No tawdry rule of kings,
But toil of serf and sweeper—
  The tale of common things.
The ports ye shall not enter,
  The roads ye shall not tread,
Go make them with your living,
  And mark them with your dead!

Take up the White Man's burden—
  And reap his old reward:
The blame of those ye better,
  The hate of those ye guard—
The cry of hosts ye humour
  (Ah, slowly) toward the light:—

'Why brought ye us from bondage,
  'Our loved Egyptian night?'

Take up the White Man's burden—
  Ye dare not stoop to less—
Nor call too loud on Freedom
  To cloak your weariness;
By all ye cry or whisper,
  By all ye leave or do,
The silent, sullen peoples
  Shall weigh your Gods and you.

Take up the White Man's burden—
  Have done with childish days—
The lightly proferred laurel,
  The easy, ungrudged praise.
Comes now, to search your manhood
  Through all the thankless years
Cold-edged with dear-bought wisdom.
  The judgment of your peers!

"The White Man's Burden (The United States and the Philippine Islands)," in Rudyard Kipling, *The Portable Kipling* (New York: Viking
Books, 1982), pp. 602–03. For an excellent commentary, see John Bellamy Foster, Harry Magdoff, and Robert W. McChesney, "Kipling, the
'White Man's Burden,' and U.S. Imperialism," in John Bellamy Foster
and Robert W. McChesney, eds., *Pox Americana: Exposing the American
Empire* (New York: Monthly Review Press, 2004), pp. 12–21.

10. Edward Rothstein, "Cherished Ideas Refracted in History's Lens," *New
York Times*, September 7, 2002, p. B11.

11. For a particularly vivid refutation of this idea, see Adam Hochschild,
*King Leopold's Ghost: A Story of Greed, Terror, and Heroism in Colonial
Africa* (New York: Mariner Books, 1999).

12. Max Boot, "The Case for American Empire," *Weekly Standard* 7, no. 5
(October 15, 2001), p. 27.

13. Niall Ferguson, "The Empire Slinks Back," *New York Times Magazine,* April 27, 2003, sec. 6, p. 54.

14. Michael Ignatieff, "Nation-Building Lite," *New York Times Magazine,* July 28, 2002, sec. 6, p. 57.

15. Michael Ignatieff, "The Burden," *New York Times Magazine,* January 5, 2003, sec. 6, p. 24. See also Michael Ignatieff, *The Lesser Evil: Political Ethics in the Age of Terror* (Princeton: Princeton University Press, 2004) and the critical review by Jeanne Morefield in *Perspectives on Politics* 3, no. 3 (September 2005), pp. 688–89. Morefield is also the author of the very useful study *Covenants Without Swords: Idealist Liberalism and the Spirit of Empire* (Princeton: Princeton University Press, 2004).

16. President George W. Bush, Remarks to the Philippines Congress, Manila, The Philippines, October 18, 2003.

17. David E. Sanger, "Bush Cites Philippines as Model in Rebuilding Iraq," *New York Times,* October 19, 2003, sec. 1, p. 1.

18. Ibid.

19. General James Rusling, "Interview with President William McKinley," *Christian Advocate,* January 22, 1903, p. 17. Reprinted in Daniel Schirmer and Stephen Rosskamm Shalom, eds., *The Philippines Reader* (Boston: South End Press, 1987), pp. 22–23. The original interview took place November 21, 1899.

20. Transcript of conversation between Henry Stimson and John J. McCloy, May 8, 1945, Stimson MSS, Box 420. Quoted in John Lewis Gaddis, *The United States and the Origins of the Cold War, 1941–1947* (New York: Columbia University Press, 1972), p. 226.

21. Clifford Kuhn, "Philippines Not a Good Model," *Atlanta Journal-Constitution,* October 22, 2003, p. 23A.

22. Mark Twain (Samuel Clemens), "Comments on the Moro Massacre," in Howard Zinn and Anthony Arnove, eds., *Voices of a People's History of the United States* (New York: Seven Stories Press, 2004), pp. 248–51.

23. See Zinn and Arnove, *Voices of a People's History of the United States,* pp. 243–47.

24. William Loren Katz, "We Are Repeating the Mistake We Made in the Philippines 100 Years Ago," History News Network, May 3, 2004. Available online at http://hnn.us/articles/4915.html.

25. See, for example, General Calixto Garcia, Letter to General William R. Shafter, July 17, 1898, in Zinn and Arnove, eds., *Voices of a People's History of the United States,* pp. 241–42.

26. Seymour M. Hersh, "The Gray Zone: How a Secret Pentagon Program Came to Abu Ghraib," *New Yorker,* May 24, 2004, p. 42. See also Emran Qureshi, "Misreading 'The Arab Mind,' " *Boston Globe,* May 30, 2004, p. D1.

4. A HISTORY OF OCCUPATION

1. William Stivers, *Supremacy and Oil: Iraq, Turkey, and the Anglo-American World Order, 1918–1930* (Ithaca: Cornell University Press, 1982), p. 7. See also Reeva Spector Simon and Eleanor H. Tejirian, eds., *The Creation of Iraq, 1914–1921* (New York: Columbia University Press, 2004), pp. 8 and 114–17.

2. Stivers, *Supremacy and Oil,* p. 7.

3. Minutes, War Cabinet 457, Imperial War Cabinet 30, August 13, 1918. British Cabinet Records 23/43. Quoted in Stivers, *Supremacy and Oil,* pp. 24–25.

4. Simon and Tejirian, eds., *The Creation of Iraq, 1914–1921,* pp. 162–63.

5. Great Britain, Foreign Office 371/6352/E 9483/100/93, August 17, 1921. Quoted in Hanna Batatu, *The Old Social Classes and the Revolutionary Movements of Iraq: A Study of Iraq's Old Landed and Commercial Classes and of Its Communists, Ba'thists, and Free Officers* (Princeton: Princeton University Press, 1978), p. 324.

6. Stivers, *Supremacy and Oil,* p. 28.

7. Eastern Committee Fifth Minutes, April 24, 1918, British Cabinet Records 27/24. Quoted in Stivers, *Supremacy and Oil,* pp. 28–29.

8. Minutes, War Cabinet 94, March 12, 1917, British Cabinet Records 23/1. Quoted in Stivers, *Supremacy and Oil,* pp. 33–34.

9. Memorandum by Lord Curzon, "German and Turkish Territories Captured in the War," December 12, 1917, British Cabinet Records. Quoted in Stivers, *Supremacy and Oil,* p. 34.

10. Stivers, *Supremacy and Oil,* pp. 68–69.

11. Eastern Committee Fifth Minutes, April 24, 1918, British Cabinet Records 27/24. Quoted in Stivers, *Supremacy and Oil,* p. 42.

12. Stivers, *Supremacy and Oil,* p. 66.

13. Robert Lansing, "Memorandum on Subjects in the President's Statement of War Aims on January 8, 1918, Which Are Open to Debate," January 10, 1918, Lansing Papers, Confidential Memoranda and Notes, vol. 1. Quoted in Stivers, *Supremacy and Oil,* p. 71.

14. Lieutenant General Sir Stanley Maude, "The Proclamation of Baghdad," March 19, 1917, Baghdad, Iraq. Reprinted in *Harper's,* May 2003, p. 31. Available online at http://www.harpers.org/ProclamationBaghdad.html. See also Robert Fisk, *The Great War for Civilisation: The Conquest of the Middle East* (New York: Alfred A. Knopf, 2005), pp. 139–49. The declaration was apparently penned by Sir Mark Sykes. For background, see Ghassan R. Atiyyah, *Iraq: 1908–1921: A Socio-Political Study* (Beirut: The Arab Institute for Research and Publishing, 1973), pp. 151–52.

15. Stivers, *Supremacy and Oil,* p. 35.

16. Cabinet Paper 1912, British Cabinet Records 24/112. Quoted in Stivers, *Supremacy and Oil,* p. 37.

17. Cabinet Paper 1790, British Cabinet Records 24/110. Quoted in Stivers, *Supremacy and Oil,* p. 37.

18. Baku Congress of the Peoples of the East, "Manifesto of the Congress to the Peoples of the East," *Kommunistichesky Internatsional,* no. 15 (December 20, 1920).

19. Winston Churchill, "British Military Liabilities," June 15, 1920, Cabinet

Paper 1467, British Cabinet Records 24/107. Quoted in Stivers, *Supremacy and Oil*, p. 39.

20. Quoted in Ilario Salucci, *A People's History of Iraq: The Iraqi Communist Party, Workers' Movements, and the Left, 1924–2004* (Chicago: Haymarket Books, 2005), p. 126.

21. Ibid.

22. Ibid.

23. Treaty of Alliance between Great Britain and Irak. Bagdad, October 10, 1922, *British and Foreign State Papers* 119: 389–94. Quoted in Stivers, *Supremacy and Oil*, p. 79.

24. Note Prepared by the Middle East Department, Colonial Office, by Instructions of the Committee, December 11, 1922, Reports, Proceedings, and Memoranda of the Cabinet Committee on Iraq, 1922–23, British Cabinet Records 27/206. Quoted in Stivers, *Supremacy and Oil*, p. 104.

25. Reports of Cabinet Committee on Iraq 3, British Cabinet Records 27/206. Quoted in Stivers, *Supremacy and Oil*, p. 105.

26. Memorandum by W.E. Perdew to Bernard Baruch, February 10, 1919, sent to the president in Paris by H.A. Garfield, March 3, 1919, Wilson Papers, series 5B. Quoted in Stivers, *Supremacy and Oil*, p. 109.

27. Postal Censorship Report No. 40, Week Ending 23 August 1919, Foreign Office 371/4197, no. E 127759. Quoted in Stivers, *Supremacy and Oil*, p. 111.

28. Samira Haj, *The Making of Iraq, 1900–1963: Capital, Power, and Ideology* (Albany: State University of New York Press, 1997), p. 80.

29. Ibid.

30. Batatu, *The Old Social Classes and the Revolutionary Movements of Iraq*, pp. 765–66.

31. Ibid., p. 764.

32. Ibid., p. 767.

33. Ibid., p. 805.

34. Haj, *The Making of Iraq, 1900–1963*, p. 80.

35. See Batatu, *The Old Social Classes and the Revolutionary Movements of*

Iraq, pp. 899 and 982–94, for a detailed discussion of this important episode.

36. Salucci, *A People's History of Iraq,* pp. 87–88.

37. The U.S. ambassador to Iraq, April Glaspie, had at best given an ambiguous cue a few days before the invasion, telling Hussein on July 25, 1990, "We have no opinion on the Arab-Arab conflicts, like your border disagreement with Kuwait," according to an Iraqi transcript. See Jim Hoagland, "Transcript Shows Muted U.S. Response to Threat by Saddam in Late July," *Washington Post,* September 13, 1990, p. A33. The U.S. government has never issued an alternate transcript disputing this statement.

38. Charles Glass, "I Blame the British," *London Review of Books* 25, no. 8 (April 17, 2003), p. 10.

5. THE RESISTANCE IN IRAQ

1. Charles Glass, "I Blame the British," *London Review of Books* 25, no. 8 (April 17, 2003), p. 10. See also the excellent article, by Susan Watkins, "Vichy on the Tigris," *New Left Review,* no. 28 (July–August 2004), pp. 5–17.

2. Rupert Cornwell, "Bush Warns Tehran to Keep Out of Iraq's Shia Strongholds," *Guardian* (London), April 24, 2003, p. 12.

3. Judith Miller, "Iraqi Dissidents Reassured in a Talk with Bush About the Post-Hussein Era," *New York Times,* January 12, 2003, sec. 1, p. 12.

4. Vice President Dick Cheney, interview with Tim Russert, *Meet the Press,* NBC, March 16, 2003.

5. Matthew Gilbert and Suzanne C. Ryan, "Snap Judgments," *Boston Globe,* April 10, 2003, p. D1.

6. Jonathan Steele, "Don't Be Fooled by the Spin on Iraq," *The Guardian* (London), April 13, 2005, p. 24.

7. Ian Fisher, "U.S. Force Said to Kill 15 Iraqis During an Anti-American Rally," *New York Times,* April 30, 2003, p. A1.

8. Richard Sisk, "Aide Could Lead U.S. to Dictator, Weapons," *Daily News* (New York), June 19, 2003, p. 7.

9. Frank Rich, "The Jerry Bruckheimer White House," *New York Times,* May 11, 2003, sec. 2, p. 1.

10. Peter Spiegel, "All Agree Insurgents Are Overwhelmingly Domestic, Sunni and Nationalist," *Financial Times* (London), January 29, 2005, p. 7. See also Edward Wong, "8 Months After U.S.-Led Siege, Insurgents Rise Again in Falluja," *New York Times,* July 15, 2005, p. A1.

11. Douglas Jehl and Neil A. Lewis, "U.S. Said to Hold More Foreigners in Iraq Fighting," *New York Times,* January 8, 2005, p. A1.

12. See figures on detainees in Jehl and Lewis, "U.S. Said to Hold More Foreigners in Iraq Fighting," p. A1.

13. Spiegel, "All Agree Insurgents Are Overwhelmingly Domestic, Sunni and Nationalist," p. 7.

14. Anthony H. Cordesman, *The Developing Iraqi Insurgency: Status at End-2004* (December 22, 2004), p. 15. See also Anthony H. Cordesman, *Iraq's Evolving Insurgency* (August 5, 2005). Both reports were published by the Center for Strategic and International Studies (http://www.csis.org).

15. Cordesman, *Iraq's Evolving Insurgency,* p. 47.

16. Gareth Porter, "How Basra Slipped Out of Control: Portent in the Shiite South?" *Foreign Policy in Focus,* October 12, 2005, p. 1.

17. Jonathan Steele and Rory McCarthy, "Sunni and Shia Unite Against Common Enemy," *The Guardian* (London), April 10, 2004, p. 5.

18. Ibid.

19. Sami Ramadani, interviewed by Eric Ruder, "Iraqis Need Our Active Solidarity," *International Socialist Review* 40 (March–April 2005), p. 29.

20. Jonathan Steele, "The Iraqi Leader Seeking a Peaceful Path to Liberation," *The Guardian* (London), July 16, 2004, p. 28.

21. Glenn Perusek, "A Horizon Lit with Blood: The U.S. Occupation and Resistance in Iraq," *New Politics* 38 (Winter 2005), pp. 48–49.

22. Dexter Filkins, "The Fall of the Warrior King," *New York Times Magazine,* October 23, 2005, sec. 6, p. 56.

23. Ramadani, "Iraqis Need Our Active Solidarity," p. 29.

24. Robert F. Worth, "2 from Tribunal for Hussein Case Are Assassinated," *New York Times,* March 2, 2005, p. A1.

25. Sameer N. Yacoub, "Anger Against Iraqi Insurgents Grows," Associated Press, March 4, 2005.

26. Traci Carl, "Iraq Workers Protest Insurgent Attacks," Associated Press, March 24, 2005.

27. Ahmed Hashim, "Terrorism and Complex Warfare in Iraq," *Terrorism Monitor* 2, no. 12 (June 17, 2004), p. 2.

28. Arundhati Roy, *Public Power in the Age of Empire* (New York: Seven Stories Press/Open Media, 2004), p. 32.

29. Tariq Ali and David Barsamian, *Speaking of Empire and Resistance: Conversations with Tariq Ali* (New York: The New Press, 2005), p. 220. See also Ali's discussion of the relationship between the character of the occupation and the nature of resistance to it (p. 228).

30. Roy, *Public Power in the Age of Empire,* p. 33. See also Tariq Ali, *Bush in Babylon: The Recolonisation of Iraq,* 2nd ed. (New York: Verso, 2004).

6. THE LOGIC OF WITHDRAWAL

1. Richard Morin and Dan Balz, "Bush's Popularity Reaches New Low," *Washington Post,* November 4, 2005, p. A1.

2. Richard Benedetto, "Bush's Approval Rating Drops to 39%, Lowest of Presidency," *USA Today,* October 18, 2005, p. 16A. Susan Page, "Mood Is Sour on Bush, Congress," *USA Today,* October 26, 2005, p. 1A.

3. Raymond Hernandez and Meegan Thee, "Iraq's Costs Worry Americans, Poll Indicates," *New York Times,* September 17, 2005, p. A1. International opposition among countries with troops in Iraq is also quite strong, according to a recent study by the Program on International Policy Attitudes. Clay Ramsay and Angela Stephens, "Among Key Iraq Partners, Weak Public Support for Troop Presence," Program on Inter-

national Policy Attitudes, October 14, 2005. Available online at http://www.pipa.org/. On British attitudes, see also Julian Glover and Michael White, "Blair Out of Step as Voters Swing Behind Iraq Withdrawal," *The Guardian* (London), September 26, 2005, p. 10.

4. Useful accounts can be found in Dilip Hiro, *Secrets and Lies: Operation "Iraqi Freedom" and After* (New York: Nation Books, 2004) and Scott Ritter, *Iraq Confidential: The Untold Story of the Intelligence Conspiracy to Undermine the UN and Overthrow Saddam Hussein* (New York: Nation Books, 2005). See also Hans Blix, *Disarming Iraq* (New York: Pantheon Books, 2004), p. 219.

5. George Gedda, "Iraqi Weapons Issue Under Wraps," Associated Press, August 16, 2000.

6. Vice President Dick Cheney, interview with Wolf Blitzer, *CNN Late Edition with Wolf Blitzer,* CNN, March 4, 2001.

7. See Declaration of the Jury of Conscience, World Tribunal on Iraq, Istanbul, Turkey, June 27, 2005 (in appendix) and Jeremy Brecher, Jill Cutler, and Brendan Smith, eds., *In the Name of Democracy: American War Crimes in Iraq and Beyond* (New York: Metropolitan Books/Henry Holt, 2005).

8. White House, *The National Security Strategy of the United States of America,* September 17, 2002. Available online at http://www.whitehouse.gov/nsc/nss.html.

9. Ronald Brownstein, "Permanent U.S. Bases in Iraq? Experts See a Political Minefield," *Los Angeles Times,* August 15, 2005, p. A8. Thom Shanker and Eric Schmitt, "Pentagon Expects Long-Term Access to Key Iraq Bases," *New York Times,* April 20, 2003, p. A1.

10. Mark Turner, "Diplomats' Diplomat Heads for Baghdad," *Financial Times* (London), June 25, 2004, p. 8. On U.S. military basing strategy, see Chalmers Johnson, *The Sorrows of Empire: Militarism, Secrecy, and the End of the Republic* (New York: Owl Books/Henry Holt, 2005).

11. Elaine Sciolino and Neil MacFarquhar, "Naming of Hijackers as Saudis May Further Erode Ties to U.S.," *New York Times,* October 25, 2001, p. A1. See also As'ad AbuKhalil, *The Battle for Saudi Arabia: Royalty, Fun-*

damentalism, and Global Power (New York: Seven Stories Press/Open Media, 2004).

12. Phyllis Bennis, "Reading the Elections," United for Peace and Justice Talking Points, no. 29 (February 1, 2005). Available online at http://www.ips-dc.org/comment/Bennis/tp29election.htm.

13. See Hana Al Bayaty, interview with David Barsamian, *International Socialist Review* 43 (September–October 2005), pp. 29–30.

14. Phyllis Bennis, "Iraq's Elections," United for Peace and Justice Talking Points, no. 27 (December 20, 2004). Available online at http://www.ips-dc.org/comment/Bennis/tp27elections.htm.

15. See Henry Kissinger, "Iraq Is Becoming Bush's Most Difficult Challenge," *Chicago Tribune,* August 11, 2002, p. 9.

16. Robert Pear and Celia W. Dugger, "Powell Tries to Ease Tension as Kashmir Pressure Builds," *New York Times,* December 27, 2001, p. A1.

17. James Bennett, "Bush's Gamble: Seeking a Delicate Balance," *New York Times,* April 5, 2002, p. A12.

18. For an excellent study of the political context of the London bombings, see Tariq Ali, *Rough Music: Blair/Bombs/Baghdad/London/Terror* (New York: Verso, 2005). On the political response to the Madrid attacks, see Amy Goodman's interview with *El País* journalist Ignacio Carrión on *Democracy Now!,* March 15, 2004.

19. "President Bush's Address on Terrorism Before a Joint Meeting of Congress," *New York Times,* September 21, 2001, p. B4.

20. See, among others, BBC World Service Poll, "In 18 of 21 Countries Polled, Most See Bush's Reelection as Negative for World Security," January 19, 2005. Available online at http://www.pipa.org/.

21. Harold Pinter, Honorary Doctorate Speech given at Turin University, Turin, Italy, November 27, 2002. Available online at http://www.haroldpinter.org/home/turinunispeech.html.

22. Greg Jaffe, "For U.S. Military, a Key Iraq Mission Is Averting Civil War," *Wall Street Journal,* October 14, 2005, p. A1.

23. Robert Fisk, "Why Is It That We and America Wish Civil War on Iraq?" *The Independent* (London), September 15, 2005, p. 2.

24. Thomas L. Friedman, "The Endgame in Iraq," *New York Times*, September 28, 2005, p. A27. Friedman has a long track record of advocating war crimes in Iraq, so this is familiar territory for him. In typically racist fashion, as always blurring the line between himself and the government with his editorial "we," he adds, "We must not throw more good American lives after good American lives for people who hate others more than they love their own children." For more on Friedman's views on Iraq, see Anthony Arnove, ed., *Iraq Under Siege: The Deadly Impact of Sanctions and War*, 2nd ed. (Cambridge: South End Press; London: Pluto Press, 2003), pp. 18–19 and 21–22. See also Friedman's belated acknowledgment of "just how devastated Iraq's society, economy and institutions had become—after eight years of war with Iran, a crushing defeat in Gulf War I and then a decade of U.N. sanctions" (Thomas L. Friedman, "What Were They Thinking?" *New York Times*, October 7, 2005, p. A29).

25. A.K. Gupta, "Unraveling Iraq's Secret Militias," *Z* 18, no. 5 (May 2005), pp. 33–37. See also A.K. Gupta, "Civil War in Iraq, Made in the USA," *Indypendent* (New York), August 4, 2005, pp. 8–9. Available online at http://nyc.indymedia.org/en/2005/08/54971.html.

26. Secretary of Defense Donald Rumsfeld, Senate Appropriations Committee, Washington, D.C., February 16, 2005. See also Anthony Shadid and Steve Fainaru, "Militias on the Rise Across Iraq," *Washington Post*, August 21, 2005, p. A1; and Shadid and Fainaru, "Kurdish Officials Sanction Abductions in Kirkuk," *Washington Post*, June 15, 2005, p. A1.

27. Phyllis Bennis, "The Iraqi Constitution: A Referendum for Disaster," United for Peace and Justice Talking Points, no. 33 (October 13, 2005). Available online at http://www.ips-dc.org/comment/Bennis/tp34constitution.htm.

28. Ibid.

29. Douglas Jehl, "Report Warned Bush Team about Intelligence Doubts," *New York Times*, November 6, 2005, sec. 1, p. 14.

30. Ibid.

31. Mark Mazzetti, "U.S. Generals Now See Virtues of a Smaller Troop Presence in Iraq," *Los Angeles Times*, October 1, 2005, p. A1.

32. Mike Allen and Sam Coates, "Bush Says U.S. Will Stay and Finish Task," *Washington Post*, August 23, 2005, p. A10.

33. Cindy Sheehan, "It's Time the Antiwar Choir Started Singing," *International Socialist Review* 43 (September–October 2005), p. 14.

34. John Kifner, James Dao, and Albert Salvato, "Confronting Their Losses, Ohio Families Are Shaken," *New York Times*, August 5, 2005, p. A7.

35. Eve Ensler, "My Son Brought Me Here," *O: The Oprah Magazine* (November 2005), p. 218.

36. Advertisements by the Halliburton Corporation, responding to such criticism, assert that the company wins contracts "because of what we do, not who we know," but its former chief executive officer from 1995 to 2000 was Dick Cheney, the vice president of the United States, and the company has a long record of receiving lucrative contracts in U.S. military zones, despite evidence of overbilling and shoddy work. See Jackie Spinner, "Halliburton to Counter Critics with Commercial," *Washington Post*, February 6, 2004, p. E3. Colum Lynch, "U.S. Owes $208 Million To Iraq, U.N. Audit Finds," *Washington Post*, November 6, 2005, p. A23. Pratap Chatterjee, *Iraq, Inc.: A Profitable Occupation* (New York: Seven Stories Press/Open Media, 2004), p. 61.

37. Charles Clover and Roula Khalaf, " 'It Was Wrong to Apply an American Template on the Iraqi Reality,' " *Financial Times* (London), October 23, 2003, p. 21. Erik Eckholm, "Excess Fuel Billing by Halliburton in Iraq Is Put at $108 Million in Audit," *New York Times*, March 15, 2005, p. A12.

38. Naomi Klein, "You Break It, You Pay for It," *The Nation*, January 10, 2005, p. 12.

39. Quoted in Norman Solomon, "MoveOn.org: Making Peace With the War in Iraq," March 10, 2005. Available online at http://www.norman-solomon.com/.

40. See, for example, the debate between Erik Gustafson and Naomi Klein on *Democracy Now!*, April 20, 2005.

41. Nicholas D. Kristof, "Saving the Iraqi Children," *New York Times*, November 27, 2004, p. A15.

42. See Noam Chomsky, *Imperial Ambitions: Conversations on the Post–9/11 World*, ed. David Barsamian (New York: Metropolitan Books/Henry Holt, 2005), pp. 115–18, and Noam Chomsky, *Hegemony or Survival: America's Quest for Global Dominance*, 2nd ed. (New York: Owl Books/Henry Holt, 2004).

43. Nicholas D. Kristof, "The Exit from Iraq," *New York Times*, November 13, 2005, sec. 4, p. 13.

44. Howard Zinn, speech with Gino Strada at Cooper Union, New York, New York, November 13, 2005.

45. U.S. officials initially denied they had used white phosphorus in Falluja, but then admitted they had. George Monbiot, "The US Used Chemical Weapons in Iraq—and then Lied About It," *The Guardian* (London), November 15, 2005, p. 31. On the broader air war, see Seymour M. Hersh, "Up in the Air," *New Yorker*, December 5, 2005, pp. 42–54. Hersh notes that "the 3rd Marine Aircraft Wing alone had dropped more than five hundred thousand tons of ordnance" on Iraq since the 2003 invasion (p. 44).

46. Mark Turner, "Iraq Force Wins Extended Mandate," *Financial Times*, November 9, 2005, p. 3. See also UN Security Council Resolution 1637 (S/RES/1637 [2005]). Available online at http://www.un.org/.

47. Serge Schmemann, "All Aboard: America's War Train Is Leaving the Station," *New York Times*, February 2, 2003, sec. 4, p. 1.

48. Klein, "You Break It, You Pay for It," p. 12. On Iraqi debt, see the detailed reports at the Jubilee Iraq web site: http://www.jubileeiraq.org/resources.htm.

7. OUT NOW

1. Richard Benedetto, "Bush Says U.S. Must Remain in Iraq," *USA Today*, October 26, 2005, p. 9A.

2. Kirk Semple and Eric Schmitt, "U.S. General Sees Further Delay

in Iraqi Military Taking Over," *New York Times,* October 22, 2005, p. A10.

3. Eric Schmitt, "Troops for All Wars; Appetite for Few," *New York Times,* October 23, 2005, p. 4: 2.

4. General John Abizaid, commander of the U.S. Central Command, testimony before the Senate Armed Services Committee, Washington, D.C., September 29, 2005.

5. Martin Sieff, "Iraq Has More Bombs but No Trained Army," United Press International, September 30, 2005.

6. Richard W. Stevenson, "Bush to Tell Why He Sees a 'Clear Path to Victory,' " *New York Times,* June 28, 2005, p. A12.

7. Richard W. Stevenson and David Sanger, "U.S. Seeks to Aid Iraqi Charter, at a Distance," *New York Times,* August 31, 2005, p. A8.

8. James Boxell, Daniel Dombey, and Demetri Sevastpoulo, "US to Retain Force in Iraq after Bush Goes," *Financial Times* (London), October 26, 2005, p. 11. See also Christopher Langton, ed., *The Military Balance 2005–2006* (London and New York: Routledge, 2006), p. 173.

9. Rumsfeld quoted in Ronald Brownstein, "Permanent U.S. Bases in Iraq? Experts See a Political Minefield," *Los Angeles Times,* August 15, 2005, p. A8. Thom Shanker and Eric Schmitt, "Pentagon Expects Long-Term Access to Key Iraq Bases," *New York Times,* April 20, 2003, p. A1.

10. Shanker and Schmitt, "Pentagon Expects Long-Term Access to Key Iraq Bases," p. A1.

11. Brownstein, "Permanent U.S. Bases in Iraq?" p. A8.

12. Scott Peterson and Dan Murphy, "Iraqis' Big Issue: US Exit Plan," *Christian Science Monitor,* January 28, 2005, p. 1.

13. Eric Schmitt, "U.S. to Withdraw All Combat Units from Saudi Arabia," *New York Times,* April 30, 2003, p. A1.

14. Quoted in David Cortright, *Soldiers in Revolt: GI Resistance During the Vietnam War,* updated ed. (Chicago: Haymarket Books, 2005), p. 3. This book, with a new introduction by Howard Zinn and new chapters by Cortright connecting Vietnam and Iraq, is indispensable to under-

standing the scope and impact of the rebellion within the U.S. armed forces during Vietnam. See also Joe Allen's multipart "History of the Vietnam War" series in *International Socialist Review*, nos. 29, 33, and 40 (available online at http://www.isreview.org/), also forthcoming as a book from Haymarket Books.

15. Amy Goodman, interview with Janis Karpinski, *Democracy Now!*, October 26, 2005.

16. Elisabeth Bumiller and Jodi Wilgoren, "Ex-Administrator's Remark Puts Bush on the Defensive," *New York Times*, October 6, 2004, p. A22. See also General Eric K. Shinseki's testimony before the Senate Armed Services Committee, Washington, D.C., February 25, 2003.

17. Eric Schmitt, "Pentagon Contradicts General on Iraq Occupation Force's Size," *New York Times*, February 28, 2003, p. A1.

18. Dexter Filkins, "The Fall of the Warrior King," *New York Times Magazine*, October 23, 2005, sec. 6, p. 56.

19. Doug Smith and P.J. Huffstutter, "A Deadly Surge," *Los Angeles Times*, October 26, 2005, p. A1.

20. Sean Rayment, "Secret MoD Poll: Iraqis Support Attacks on British Troops," *Sunday Telegraph* (London), October 23, 2005, p. 1. The study also found that 82 percent of Iraqis "strongly oppose" the occupation troops and 67 percent feel less secure because of the occupation, while only 1 percent feel more secure.

21. Sabrina Tavernise, "Unseen Enemy Is at Its Fiercest in a Sunni City," *New York Times*, October 23, 2005, sec. 1, p. 1.

22. Will Dunham, "U.S. Faces Grim Forecast for Army Recruitment," Reuters, October 1, 2005.

23. Demetri Sevastopulo, "Recruiters in Fierce Battle to Hit Targets for Enlistment," *Financial Times* (London), June 1, 2005, p. 10.

24. James Dao, "2,000 Dead: As Iraq Tours Stretch On, a Grim Mark," *New York Times*, October 26, 2005, p. A1.

25. For two useful overviews, see Anya Kamenetz, "Coalition of the Unwilling," *Village Voice*, October 28, 2005, p. 39, and Elizabeth Wrigley-Field,

"A New Battleground on Campuses," ZNet, June 18, 2005 (available online at www.zmag.org).

26. Damien Cave, "Growing Problem for Military Recruiters: Parents," *New York Times*, June 3, 2005, p. A1.

27. See Elizabeth Weill-Greenberg, ed., *Ten Excellent Reasons Not to Join the Military* (New York: The New Press, 2006) and Tod Ensign, ed., *America's Military Today: The Challenge of Militarism* (New York: The New Press, 2005).

28. Dan Rather, interview with Camilo Mejía, CBS, *60 Minutes II,* March 31, 2004. Suzanne Goldenberg, "The Stand," *The Guardian* (London), May 5, 2004, sec. G2, p. 6. See Camilo Mejía, *The Road from Ar Ramadi* (New York: The New Press, 2006).

29. Joe Garofoli, "Anti-War Sailor Lifts Foes of Iraq Policy," *San Francisco Chronicle*, May 28, 2005, p. B1. Stuart Cashin, "War Objector Simply Put Conscience First," *Atlanta Journal-Constitution*, August 10, 2005, p. 11A.

30. Paolo Pontoniere, Pacific News Service, "Deserters Speak Out," *Chicago Sun-Times,* July 31, 2005, p. 5.

31. Phillip O'Connor, "Some Just Say No to Iraq Duty," *Saint Louis Post-Dispatch,* February 20, 2005, p. A1.

32. John F. Worth, "Army Punishes 23 for Refusing Convoy Order," *New York Times,* December 7, 2004, p. A12.

33. Eric Schmitt and Ariel Hart, "Punishment Urged for Reservists Who Disobeyed," *New York Times,* November 16, 2004, p. A13. Celeste Katz, " 'All of Us Refused to Go,' " *Daily News* (New York), October 17, 2004, p. 7.

34. See Table 1 (page xx) and sources.

35. Mark Mulligan, "Spanish Premier Gives Pledge on Troops," *Financial Times* (London), May 12, 2005, p. 10.

36. Pew Global Attitudes Project, "Global Opinion: The Spread of Anti-Americanism," *Trends 2005* (Washington, D.C.: Pew Research Center, 2005), pp. 113–27. See summary at http://pewglobal.org/commentary/display.php?AnalysisID=104.

37. See, for example, William J. Holstein, "Erasing the Image of the Ugly American," *New York Times,* October 23, 2005, sec. 3, p. 9.

38. William E. Odom, "What's Wrong with Cutting and Running?" Nieman Watchdog Journalism Project, Nieman Foundation for Journalism at Harvard University, August 3, 2005. Available online at http://www.niemanwatchdog.org. The article was also reprinted as "Now's the Time to Leave Iraq," *Pittsburgh Post-Gazette,* September 18, 2005, p. K1.

39. Richard Morin and Dan Balz, "Bush's Popularity Reaches New Low," *Washington Post,* November 4, 2005, p. A1.

40. Rasmussen Reports, "23% Belong to Anti-War Movement," September 28, 2005. Available online at http://www.rasmussenreports.com/2005/Anti-War%20Movement.htm. Based on Population Estimates Program as of July 1, 2005. For U.S. Census figures sorted by demographics, see http://www.census.gov/popest/age.html.

41. Table 2 used with permission of The Harris Poll.

42. David E. Sanger, "Hard New Test for President," *New York Times,* September 1, 2005, p. A1.

43. James Harding, "Kerry Avoids Anti-War Campaigning," *Financial Times* (London), May 12, 2004, p. 9. Harding observed at the time that "the latest polls tell an 'impossible, but true' story: both Mr. Bush and Mr. Kerry are losing the 2004 presidential election." An apt metaphor. In the end, Bush barely defeated Kerry, among those who bothered to participate in an election with two prowar candidates competing for votes from a population that had turned against the war.

44. Jim VandeHei, "In Hindsight, Kerry Says He'd Still Vote for War," *Washington Post,* August 10, 2004, p. A1. For his later, pathetic, retraction, see Dana Milbank, "An Iraq Policy, Better Late Than Never," *Washington Post,* October 27, 2005, p. A3.

45. Peter Baker and Shailagh Murray, "Democrats Split over Position on Iraq War," *Washington Post,* August 22, 2005, p. A1.

46. Joseph I. Lieberman, "Lieberman on Iraq, Judge Roberts, Party Politics," *Hartford Courant,* August 14, 2005, p. C6.

47. Raymond Hernandez and Patrick D. Healy, "From Seeking Major Change at Once to Taking Small Steps," *New York Times,* July 13, 2005, p. B1.

48. Charles Babington, "Hawkish Democrat Joins Call For Pullout," *Washington Post,* November 18, 2005, p. A1. See also Gilbert Achcar and Stephen R. Shalom, "On John Murtha's Position," ZNet, November 21, 2005 (available online at www.zmag.org). Achcar and Shalom rightly note that Murtha's position is a strategy for redeployment of U.S. troops in the Middle East. Murtha, in fact, voted against a resolution for immediate withdrawal, which only three Democrats had the courage to support. Murtha comes from the defense establishment, as Seymour Hersh noted on *Democracy Now!,* on November 29, 2005. Indeed, he is the leading congressional recipient, by far, of money from the space weapons lobby. See William D. Hartung et al., *Tangled Web 2005: A Profile of the Missile Defense and Space Weapons Lobbies* (New York: Arms Trade Resource Center, 2005), Tables III and IV.

49. Jeremy Scahill, "Vegetarians Between Meals: This War Cannot Be Stopped by a Loyal Opposition," Common Dreams.org, November 18, 2005.

50. Rick Klein, "Democrats Embrace Tough Military Stance," *Boston Globe,* August 14, 2005, p. A1.

51. Samih Farsoun, "Roots of the American Antiterrorism Crusade," in Elaine C. Hagopian, ed., *Civil Rights in Peril: The Targeting of Arabs and Muslims* (Chicago: Haymarket Books, 2004), pp. 133–60. See also Mahmood Mamdani, *Good Muslim, Bad Muslim: America, the Cold War, and the Roots of Terror* (New York: Pantheon Books, 2004) and Tariq Ali, *The Clash of Fundamentalisms: Crusades, Jihad and Modernity,* 2nd ed. (New York: Verso, 2003). On Islam more generally, see Gilbert Achcar, *Eastern Cauldron: Islam, Afghanistan, Palestine, and Iraq in a Marxist Mirror* (New York: Monthly Review Press, 2004) and Paul N. Siegel, *The Meek and the Militant: Religion and Power Across the World* (Chicago: Haymarket Books, 2005).

52. Yaroslav Trofimov, "In a Tent Hospital, a Close-Up View of Attacks in Iraq," *Wall Street Journal,* October 29, 2003, p. A1.

53. See Howard Zinn and Anthony Arnove, *Voices of a People's History of the United States.* (New York: Seven Stories Press, 2004), p. 248.

54. Steve Negus, "Baghdad to Start Lifting Petrol Subsidies," *Financial Times,* October 28, 2005, p. 7.

55. Howard Zinn, *Terrorism and War,* ed. Anthony Arnove (New York: Seven Stories Press/Open Media, 2003), p. 37.

56. Ibid., p. 38.

57. Susan Milligan, "GAO Investigator Rips Pentagon on Iraq War Finances," *Boston Globe,* July 15, 2005, p. A4.

58. Reuters, "House Passes $409 Billion in Defense Spending," *Washington Post,* June 21, 2005, p. A8.

59. See Hagopian, ed., *Civil Rights in Peril,* for many examples.

60. International Brotherhood of Teamsters Local 705, Resolution Against the War, October 18, 2002. Reprinted in Zinn and Arnove, eds., *Voices of a People's History of the United States,* p. 608.

61. Joseph Carroll, "Who Says It Was a Mistake to Send Troops to Iraq?" Gallup Poll, November 1, 2005. Available online at http://poll.gallup.com/content/default.aspx?ci=10024.

62. Ibid.

63. NBC News–*Wall Street Journal* poll, October 12, 2005. Tim Russert and Brian Lehrer, *NBC Nightly News,* NBC, October 12, 2005.

64. From the original text of the speech John Lewis intended to deliver at the march on Washington, August 28, 1963. In Zinn and Arnove, *Voices of a People's History of the United States,* p. 399.

AFTERWORD: ON AMERICAN EXCEPTIONALISM

1. John Winthrop, "A Model of Christian Charity," sermon delivered on voyage to Plymouth, quoted in Stuart Rosenblum, ed., *Pragmatism and Religion* (Chicago: University of Illinois Press, 2003), pp. 21–23.

2. Ronald Reagan, Acceptance Speech, Republican National Convention, Dallas, Texas, August 23, 1984.

3. William Bradford, *History of Plimoth Plantation,* ed. William T. Davis, in *Bradford's History of Plymouth Plantation, 1606–1646* (New York: Charles Scribner's Sons, 1908), pp. 339–40.

4. John O'Sullivan, "Annexation" *U.S. Magazine and Democratic Review* 17, no. 85 (July–August 1845), p. 5.

5. General James Rusling, "Interview with President William McKinley," *Christian Advocate,* January 22, 1903, p. 17. Reprinted in Daniel Schirmer and Stephen Rosskamm Shalom, eds., *The Philippines Reader* (Boston: South End Press, 1987), pp. 22–23. The date of the original interview was November 21, 1899.

6. Arnon Regular, "Road Map Is a Life Saver for Us, PM Abbas Tells Hamas," *Ha'aretz,* June 24, 2003.

7. Henry R. Luce, "The American Century," *Life* (February 17, 1941), pp. 61–65.

8. Henry Cabot Lodge, "Our Blundering Foreign Policy," *Forum* (March 1895), p. 8.

9. Elihu Root, "The American Soldier," speech given at the Marquette Club, Chicago, Illinois, October 7, 1899, in Robert Bacon and James Brown Scott, eds., *The Military and Colonial Policy of the United States: Addresses and Reports by Elihu Root* (Cambridge: Harvard University Press, 1916), p. 3.

10. Woodrow Wilson, speech at Convention Hall in Philadelphia, Pennsylvania, May 10, 1915, quoted in Arthur S. Link, *Wilson: The Struggle for Equality, 1914–1915* (Princeton: Princeton University Press, 1960), p. 382.

11. Humphrey proposed this in the debates around the McCarran Act (also known as the Internal Security Act) of 1950, opposing the act on the grounds that it did not go far enough.

12. Editorial, "The State of Bush's Union," *Boston Globe,* January 30, 1991, p. 14.

13. Steven Greenhouse, "U.S. Says Iraq Appears to Resume Pullback From Kuwait Border," *New York Times*, October 17, 1994, p. A10.

14. Henry Kissinger, "Iraq Is Becoming Bush's Most Difficult Challenge," *Chicago Tribune*, August 11, 2002, p. 9.

15. Paul Starr, Michael Tomasky, and Robert Kuttner, "The Liberal Uses of Power," *American Prospect*, March 5, 2005, p. 21.

16. President George W. Bush, Remarks to the Philippines Congress, Manila, The Philippines, October 18, 2003.

17. Secretary of State Colin Powell, Remarks with Mexican Foreign Minister Luis Ernesto Derbez, November 12, 2003.

18. Kevin Sullivan, "Mexican Envoy, a Critic of U.S., Is Fired," *Washington Post*, November 19, 2003, p. A23.

19. Elisabeth Bumiller and Richard W. Stevenson, "Bush, at 2nd Inaugural, Says Spread of Liberty is the 'Calling of Our Time,' " *New York Times*, January 21, 2005, p. A1.

20. Photo by Chris Hondros/Getty Images. *New York Times*, January 19, 2005, p. A10.

21. From Turkish paper *Hurriyet*, quoted in Edward Cody, "China, Others Criticize U.S. Report on Rights," *Washington Post*, March 4, 2005, p. A14.

22. Michael Gawenda, "Fresh Evidence of CIA Torture Network," *Sydney Morning Herald*, March 8, 2005.

23. Albert Einstein, quoted in Alfred Lief, ed., *The Fight Against War* (New York: John Day, 1933), p. 37.

24. See Henry Mayer, *All on Fire: William Lloyd Garrison and the Abolition of Slavery* (New York: St. Martin's Press, 1998), p. 111.

INDEX